MW01265115

"Few people like to talk abou[t] [failures], [they cover them] up, sweep them under the rug, [...] discovered a better way. Failure is a powerful path forward; we need only change our perspective on it. Justin's writing is full of helpful stories and lessons of faith. To really succeed, you must learn how to fail well. Justin will show you the way."

Chase Replogle, Pastor and Author of *The 5 Masculine Instincts*

"This amazing book is not only a road map for how to elevate your career but is a much needed reminder in how to rise up as a human being! Justin poignantly reveals the power of shifting your mindset when it comes to failure and mentorship. While we often connect with others while celebrating success, it's equally meaningful to form a kinship in the face of failure. Such an important lesson!"

John Lohrenz, Author of *The Prosperity Project*

"Justin Skinner delivers an exceptional perspective on how to learn from not just our own failures, but the failures of others. As someone who has extensive experience with failure, I'm truly grateful for the simple and powerful lessons provided in Professional Failure. They are lessons we can all benefit from."

Adam Hill, Performance Coach and Author of *Shifting Gears*

"Professional Failure is a remarkable book that reminds us failure is not something to fear, but a powerful tool for growth. Justin conveys real world wisdom through the lens of engaging stories. If you're looking to improve your life, then this book will be your mentor and guide on your path to personal growth."

Erik Hardy, Author of *The Being Equation*

Professional
failure

using the gift of failures
to better yourself and
those around you

JUSTIN SKINNER

© 2022 by Justin Skinner

All rights reserved. No part of this publication may be reproduced or transmitted in any form or by any means, electronic or mechanical, including photography, recording, or any information storage and retrieval system, without permission in writing from the author.

Requests for permission to make copies of any part of the work should be mailed to the following address:
justin@professional-failure.com

www.professional-failure.com

Published and distributed by Merack Publishing.

Library of Congress Control Number: 2022902624
Skinner, Justin, 1985

Paperback ISBN 978-1-957048-19-2
Hardcover ISBN 978-1-957048-21-5

Cover design: Justin and Kendra Skinner
Author photo: Kendra Skinner

This book is dedicated to my beautiful wife, Kendra.
Without you, life would be much less colorful. Your spiritual
wisdom and connectedness challenges me in ways that no
one else can. I love you more than anything on this earth.

And may this book point others to Jesus Christ.
*Without Him, I would simply not have life. I strive to not
waste my short time I've been given. Let this book be a
small tool in the building of His kingdom.*

T A B L E
of
C O N T E N T S

INTRODUCTION

This book is an expression of gratitude for all those who have invested time into not only teaching me but giving me the opportunity to fail. Through these failures I've learned the value of effort. Without effort, I simply would not be where I am today.

The goal of this book is not to be better for just yourself and your selfish ambitions, but to ultimately be better for those around you. You want to become a resource to those around you and give in abundance. You want to be extravagant in the giving of your time, knowledge, and money, which all comes from an overflow of you. Connect with true knowledge and power, fill your heart with truth and wisdom, and let that overflow into others' lives around you. Simple in theory, complex and difficult in execution.

I also want to make a point that I revisit concepts throughout the book. The main thoughts are intertwined throughout each concept. Just as repetition in sports sometimes takes a while before you get the hang of things, the same goes with learning. Sometimes a new concept needs to be heard multiple times before it truly sinks in and you are able to put it into motion.

More than anything, this book is focused on the gift of failures. People often talk about learning from your own failures, which is an amazing tool and mindset to possess. But after mastering that mindset, we can take it a step further. What if we shifted our focus to learning from other people's failures as well as our own? What if we could tap into a rare mindset that would allow us to advance our growth, and the growth of those around us, at an extraordinary rate? It can be done, and it has been done throughout history—you just may not realize it. It takes a different viewpoint, courage, and a lot of discipline, all of which you can develop and grow into yourself. Learning from your own mistakes is a great asset and should be used daily, but it can also be a slow process. You can only learn so much in one given experience, day, or month. But when you leverage other individuals' minds, who draw from their own experiences, you can assess their actions, take note, and learn at a much faster pace. You may already mindlessly do this and don't understand just how incredibly powerful it is.

One of the greatest byproducts of learning from your mistakes and becoming better yourself is that you also develop the ability to mentor others. The goal is to help them avoid the same mistakes you made, increase their chances of success, and give them a better foundation to build from. However, without having intimate knowledge of the subject you're teaching, it can be difficult to connect with someone on a meaningful and impactful level. You may teach, but without experience in the subject matter, it can be hard for the pupil to fully trust you and learn. For example, if I were to teach someone about the fundamentals of hitting a baseball, I could draw from the moments that I lived out those fundamentals. I could also provide examples of my successes and failures in my playing days and could connect with someone on a different level versus someone who has never played the game of baseball. On the other hand, if I were to teach someone how to rebuild a car, I would have no expertise or experience to share. I would be simply regurgitating what I have read or watched but never experienced myself. The level of mentorship is completely different. It's very difficult to be a great mentor in areas where you have no experience. You have the opportunity to learn from a multitude of mentors in many different subjects, but you can only be a mentor for a select few. Experience is vital when it comes to mentorship. We will explore the lost art of mentorship later in this book.

One of the greatest byproducts of learning from other people's mistakes is the value you bring to those lives. Whether it is simply listening to their small nugget of wisdom, or reading their life's work, you give purpose and meaning to the mistakes they've made. You allow them to see that their mistakes were not made in vain and can serve a greater purpose. Missteps and shortcomings can have an impact on the success of future generations. This is powerful and can create bonds that are not easily broken. If you take the time to listen to someone sharing wisdom and then take additional time to implement what he is sharing, it can be deeply meaningful to him. Remember that next time you're speaking with your grandparents or the old man on the corner. Listen and pay attention. There is wisdom all around us, we just have to have the ears and eyes to comprehend.

Interestingly enough, it doesn't even matter if you actually make the mistakes yourself, it only matters that you recognize the mistake. Seek to not repeat it or do it yourself. You can give meaning to someone's life by simply giving credit where credit is due. When someone teaches you a lesson, be aware and include her in your accomplishment or success. After all, it's not your success alone and never will be. We are all made up of bits and pieces of lessons learned from those around us.

Furthermore, when in competition, whether it be work or play, you can compete at a high level and root wholeheartedly for the people you're competing against. You don't have to root for injury or fatigue, but that they compete at a high level. I know there are plenty of people that are motivated by creating adversity in their own minds. Normally that adversity or adversary is the person or team they are competing against. They become the evil figure that needs to be defeated. They are dehumanized and are nothing more than a roadblock in your way to victory. But I would strongly propose that there is a better way. If you fully lean into a growth mindset (which we will talk about later in this book) and you wish the best for the other person, you can rise together. Not only will your counterpart become better, but you will be forced to rise to his/her level and become better yourself. If you don't, you will simply be left behind.

You can actually be friendly with those you compete against. It is possible to encourage one another through competition. It is possible to wish for your counterparts to play well and for you to just outperform them. You will begin to win, even when you lose. You will undoubtedly fail in competition, in large and small ways, but refocusing that anger and disappointment of failure in a positive way is the key. That refocusing and redirecting is the key to so much in our lives. There is nothing wrong with competing and striving to win, but when you make enemies along the way, what good does it bring you? You may achieve fame and riches, but in the end, you'll end up alone. If that's your goal, and you don't care about being alone, then this book probably won't make sense to you. But you need to understand that you don't have to trample over people on your way up. You can build others up along the way and allow yourself to go further than you could ever go at it alone. And if you're playing a team sport, you can use this same mindset to make your team better–significantly better.

If you want to become a catalyst for success and encourage those who play with and against you, then keep reading. This mindset is the secret that shouldn't be a secret. It should be shared with everyone around you that will listen. And it's not just for competition; it can be implemented in your place of work and your place of skill. Some people will think it's dumb and won't listen, and that's perfectly acceptable. That's where courage comes in. You will never be able to please everyone, but you can try to add value to other people's lives–whether they accept it or not. You can become great and also make others around you great. It doesn't have to be one or the other.

A great example of a professional failure is Emmitt Smith. Emmitt is a Hall of Fame running back that played for the Dallas Cowboys. He won three super bowls and an MVP while with the Cowboys. He has talked about how he was mentored at a young age and always sought to have mentors in his life. Emmitt has also spoken about how if he didn't know an answer to a question or how to do something, he never hesitated to reach out to someone for advice. He had the humility to ask for help. This is one of the greatest abilities Emmitt Smith possesses. It wasn't his strength or agility (even though they were off the charts) but his mental ability to be humble and learn. Even when he was dominating on the football field, he could focus on his future after football as well. He was able to play at the highest level in the present but also be well aware of the future.

At a Mentor Tech event in 2017, Emmitt said, *"It's funny how life itself, and the journey and whole process of life itself, take you places that you never thought you would go."*[1] This statement refers to all the opportunities that he came across during his playing days and after he was done. He just kept learning and growing and opportunities came to him. He kept asking questions and getting advice from experienced coaches and mentors. He never settled or thought he knew everything, in football or life. Emmitt later reached out to guys like Jerry Jones, Roger Staubach, and Magic Johnson for help with investments and life after professional sports.[2]

Emmitt Smith has always helped other entrepreneurs and people, as well. He started a charity with his former wife, Pat, that helped disadvantaged children receive educational opportunities. He is always willing to help coach people through business decisions and investment directions. In no way is he perfect, but when it comes to learning from one's own failures and the failures of others, Emmitt Smith is someone to look up to. He knows how to be patient, recognize wisdom in others, and implement their teachings into his own life.

I wrote this book to compile and share the many teachings and lessons I've learned so far from some pretty amazing people. My hope is that you will read this book, find encouragement, and pass that encouragement on to others. You can use that newfound courage to help propel your life forward and provide value to those around you. Let's get started!

Chapter One

THE MAIN INGREDIENTS

"An intelligent person learns from their own mistakes, but a genius learns from the mistakes of others."

- Anonymous

Everything in my life is based on two basic fundamentals and one mission. This is the lens that I view the entire world, both physically and spiritually. These foundational principles are in place to drive every decision and possible reaction along the journey. I'm definitely not perfect in my pursuit to follow them, but they are there to guide me. The fundamentals are to love your neighbor as yourself and love the Lord God with all your heart. These simple, yet wise and edifying teachings come directly from the Bible. Lucky for me, my parents taught me this early on. Mastering these two fundamentals will lead to a life of purpose and fulfillment. Using these teachings as a guide on your journey will bring joy and many opportunities. It's not a matter of being less so those around you can be more but a matter of being your absolute best, so you can improve and be a blessing to the lives of others.

In striving to live out these two fundamentals, I am again far from perfect. There are many times when I fall short. There are many times when I don't treat people the way I should. However, I don't beat myself up for my shortcomings. I try, fail, learn, and then hopefully improve so I don't make the same mistakes again. In order to learn, I need to see my failures from different angles. This is a great example of why I need great people around me that can speak truth and life into situations. The circle you have around you is incredibly important. The company you keep is vital to your success and well-being, both physically and mentally. You need wise and caring people around you to live the life of a professional failure. Great people speak truth and wisdom into your failures, not lies and deceit.

Beyond these two fundamentals, I have a heartfelt mission and discipline to be a resource. Not to just make money for me, but to be a resource in life that people can turn to when they have questions: questions regarding business, money, life, and many other things. I want to be an open-source platform that exists to better those around me. I once heard a pastor say that when God pours out blessings, people around that person receive overflow blessings. I want to be an abundance of blessings to help guide others and motivate them to do the same.

Loving your neighbor as yourself is not easy. It might be simple, but it's not easy. It's not easy to love your neighbors when they don't see things the way you do. It's not easy when they have different political views. It's not easy when they're disrespectful and try to bully you around.

You are not required to get along with all people, and there will always be someone who doesn't like you. I've come to understand that's just a part of life. It's definitely not easy, but with an eternal perspective in mind and a perspective of learning and growth, it's more than worth the effort. You will show your neighbors respect by seeking to learn from them. You will give them value by asking questions and listening. You don't have to agree on every level with others to learn from them. In fact, I don't know anyone that I agree with 100% of the time, not even my wonderful wife or God-fearing parents. Once you realize this, it can be easier to look past the faults of others and see them for the gifts they can be. I will repeat this often, but it cannot be said enough: no one is perfect. That status is not attainable. Learn to see and value people's imperfections in order to treasure the amazing abilities and talents they offer.

It's also not easy to love God with all your heart all the time. It's not easy to be grateful to God when seasons are overwhelming and depleting. It's not easy to love God when you don't get what you think you need. Again, it's not easy, but it's worth the effort. What I've come to realize is that God sees things in a different way than you and I. Just because we don't understand what He's doing, doesn't mean He's not working and trustworthy. When you realize this truth, it can be easier to allow God to open and close doors for you. Doors that you think should be opening, don't open. Doors that make no worldly sense and should be closed, sometimes open. Lean into this. It becomes a little easier to trust and be grateful for the difficult seasons in your life.

The hard times will come, but if you can endure them with the right mindset, the hard times often produce the best fruit. Trials and tribulations provide the best learning opportunities to take to heart and pass along lessons learned to others in desperate need. Loving God with all your heart takes discipline and consistent trust. In the end, it's worth the effort.

When I seek to be the resource I desire to be, I desperately need wisdom. Not just knowledge, but Godly wisdom from other people's unique experiences and musings. I seek this through conversations, books, podcasts, and the Bible. Without wise content flowing through your mind, it's nearly impossible to be a good resource. Just as simplicity is often the apex in design, true wisdom is actually simplicity in its greatest form. True wisdom is being able to take a complex thought and communicate it in a way that anyone can understand. If you are truly wise, you are figuring out the puzzle and showing someone where the pieces are. You're taking a 1000 piece puzzle and turning it into a 10 piece puzzle to share. The mentee receiving wisdom then has put the pieces together for themselves. Effort is needed on both sides.

Wisdom is being able to know the entire dictionary and then simplifying it down to everyday words for anyone to understand. What good does wisdom do for you if you never pass it along and share it with others? It can easily become an idol and can be held over people for selfish gain. The, "I'm greater than you because I know more than you," mentality is not wisdom; it's acting like a pharisee and trumpeting your intelligence. It's acting like someone that's insecure and has to put others down to lift himself up. Don't be a pharisee. You're better than that.

ABUNDANCE MINDSET

Success is defined differently from person to person, but whatever the ultimate goal may be, an abundance mindset is critical. This simple concept can change the world. I'm not just talking casually about changing the world as many do, but actually taking the steps to do it. If in your mind you have something to share, whether it be money or wisdom, you can joyfully pass this along to others and lift them up to become more successful themselves. It's an endless loop. The more you give, the more you can receive. You can be highly successful and still place your neighbor ahead of yourself. It's not one or the other.

What does an abundant mindset look like? Someone with an abundant mindset is an overall optimist and is genuinely happy for others when they achieve some level of success. This individual knows when someone else is enjoying success, it's not just a one-off event. There is plenty of success to go around. Success is not finite but rather infinite. Most people don't understand this and focus on what they need to become successful. When your attention turns to helping others achieve, you build on the endless supply of success. The supply will never run dry. If everyone on the planet shared in successful moments, there would be no scarcity of success but rather a building of community and positivity. The world would look a lot different and ultimately be a better place.

On the contrary, someone with a scarcity mindset sees a finite amount of success in the world and tends to be jealous of others' success. This person thinks if someone is experiencing success, that means she has taken it from someone else. That's a boldfaced lie directly from the devil. This is detrimental not only to your growth but also to the growth of others around you. It's difficult to be around people who have a scarcity mindset. They tend to take from others, whether it be money, knowledge, or time, and often only share when it benefits them. When you think of a positive and uplifting person to be around, it's generally not someone with a scarcity mindset.

An abundant mindset is often applied to money, but it can be just as applicable to wisdom. I remember being around my grandpa growing up in Missouri. He was a wise man, but he never made you feel dumb for your lack of knowledge. He was a reserved listener, but when you invited his wisdom into your life with a question, he would open up his database of knowledge. He knew an incredible amount about farming and plants, so much that he could have written books on the different subjects. One simple question to him about a type of tree would lead to an abundant education session. Even though he was busy with the farm, he seemed to always have time to answer a question.

How did my grandpa become so knowledgeable? He gained his wisdom through experience, reading, and constantly learning. I remember him still reading magazines and learning new farming techniques as he was entering his 80's and 90's. He was filling himself with practical knowledge so he could confidently pass it along at the right time. He was then more than able to pass that wisdom along to others, wanting nothing more than a good conversation in return.

People with this abundant mindset tend to have a heightened ability to continue learning. Hopefully, they're passing that knowledge along to others as they learn and grow. People with an abundance mindset don't see knowledge and wisdom as something to be protected and held onto for their own selfish gain. There's no need to store up wisdom to use it as a weapon against others. People who share wisdom freely don't have to be know-it-alls, but if someone asks and is willing to take the time to learn, they share. It's a tricky balance, and that's why it's so hard to execute. People don't like know-it-alls. They're arrogant and off-putting. However, freely sharing wisdom and experience with others (when they ask) goes beyond the know-it-all mentality.

It comes from a place of humility and with the intent of adding value to the other person. Make it a goal to add value to people's lives. It creates an infinite return. A return you might not see right away, but like planted seeds, the fruit will come later. There is more wisdom in this world (and beyond) than anyone can ever hold at one time. It doesn't matter how smart you think you are, no one has the capacity to learn everything. Even if someone tried to accumulate every ounce of knowledge available, he would run out of time. We are all mortals, and we will all eventually die. With that in mind, why not share as much as you possibly can, helping others along the way, and in turn, gaining wisdom yourself? As the saying goes, "When the student is ready, the teacher appears." Students with an abundant mindset will grow exponentially. They will open their eyes to see all that's available around them and the endless opportunities to grow and become a better version of themselves. And then one day, they will become teachers. It's a beautiful cycle.

Let's also look at the other side, which is a scarcity mindset. For example, if you have one pie and someone asks you to share, resources are scarce. You only have one pie to share. Once it's gone, there isn't anything else to share. You're more stingy with how you share and who you share with. This can easily lead to greed and possessiveness. This benefits only you (on the surface) and will not benefit others. For most people, this is how they view capitalism and making money. They make money at the cost of someone else. There's only so much to go around and once it's gone, it can no longer be made. This is dangerous thinking. When contemplating a scarcity mindset and how it pertains to wisdom, it's even more dangerous. When people withhold knowledge on a subject or general wisdom, they are essentially holding power over others. They often don't want them to share the same level of thinking, either because they have a higher position in a company, or are older, therefore they should be more experienced. This damages relationships and potential in other people. The goal should be to lift each other up, not beat others down.

A scarcity mindset will be detrimental to you and those around you in the long run. It only empowers the individual on the surface. When a person wants, he/she takes a finite resource from someone else. There's not enough to go around and there's no reason to share with someone who doesn't deserve it. On the contrary, an abundance mindset will lead to greater success within yourself and others. It will build relationships. It's a short-term trade-off for a long-term gain, and it's a win-win situation. The infinite flow of knowledge and wisdom is where freedom lies for you and those around you. Make a conscious effort to freely pass along wisdom when others ask, and you'll soon discover the limitless benefits of an abundance mindset!

THE ELUSIVE MINDSET

One of the hardest things to break free from is how you view the world. We are beautifully created, but we are made up of little habits and triggers based largely on our upbringing. How we interact with certain subjects, both physically and mentally, also plays a big part. If you get your mind right, there are very few things you can't accomplish. If you believe you are worthy and ready, you will be worthy and ready. Just like an individual's definition of success can be different from others (and not necessarily wrong), mindsets can vary as well. That is the beauty of individuals and freedom of thought. But for the context of this book, we are specifically talking about the elusive mindset of learning and growing rapidly from mistakes: learning from your own mistakes and, more importantly, learning from the mistakes of others.

If you can train your brain to see the potential of a situation rather than viewing it as a hindrance, you will have unlocked a world of possibilities! It's like having access to a secret room. You don't have to have a key, you just need to know where to find it. Learn to embrace the hard times, because it's the hard times that lead to a bountiful harvest.

Let's play out a made-up scenario and break it down with two different mindsets. The day starts off fine, but when you go from your bedroom to your kitchen, you trip over a shoe that you left in front of the door. It angers you, so you kick it out of the way and wake your spouse. When you go to start your coffee, you realize that you forgot to buy more coffee filters. No coffee for you this morning! You fumble through your clothing choices and realize you're out of socks. You need socks, so you wear a dirty pair that doesn't smell that bad. You rush out the door and get in your car. You back up in a hurry and forget that your spouse parked behind you this time. You smash into her car and damage both vehicles. You sprint back into the house to grab the other set of keys but can't find them. At this point, you're frantic and losing your cool. After five minutes that seem like thirty, you locate the keys and move the other car out of the way. You'll deal with that mess later. You're finally on the road and reach work late. Your boss isn't happy because you didn't text or call to inform him that you would be late. You also forgot to eat and are very hungry. You grab a donut from the break room and gobble it down without breathing. One hour later, you're tired and ready to call it a day, but you still have a full day of work left.

Here's where the differences in mindsets become evident. The first mindset is seeing events and happenings as a hindrance and annoyance. Bad things happen to you because you're just unlucky and things will probably never change. It was just another awful Monday morning that happens all too often. You think to yourself, *"There was nothing I could have done. It wasn't my fault."* The random shoe and the absence of coffee filters are your spouse's fault, as she was supposed to take care of those. The sock monster ate my sock–they're always randomly disappearing! The car parked behind you and the temporarily lost keys are also clearly your spouse's fault. Excuses are in abundance, and you're not any better for it. If you want your future to be different, you need a new mindset.

The elusive mindset is learning in the moment coupled with learning retrospectively. After you stumble over the shoe, you know you need to not ignore that you saw it the night before and assumed your spouse would take care of it. That's your fault. Lesson one. When you realize you're out of coffee filters, you need to think to yourself, "It would be wise to always have a backup stash of filters somewhere in the house for emergencies." Lesson two. When you can't find any clean socks, you realize that you should probably be more proactive the night before and prepare for the next day. Lesson Three. Check your rear-view mirror before backing up. Always. Lesson four. When you're late, it's kind to let your boss know so he's not worried about where you are. Lesson five. After your tired spell at work, you're now thinking donuts probably aren't the best energy source and long-term healthy break-fast go-to. Lesson six. There are valuable lessons all around us, and that's just from things that have happened to you. Now imagine the conversation you could have with your coworker at lunch about what happened to her last week. Think of her story in the same way. What lessons can you learn from her without having to actually experience the mess she had to deal with? Once you are able to switch your frame of mind, you can then learn to take action. And remember, knowing is not enough–you must put what you've learned into practice for it to make an impact in your life and those around you.

A friend once sent me a video of Rick Warren's personal book collection at his home. He was standing in his library when he grabbed a book. The library was large with many beautiful wooden shelves, all filled with books. Any reader would be proud to have this as his study. The man opened the book and pressed a button. A secret door opened into another room. This room was massive with rows and rows of books on each side and a walkway in the middle. It looked like a public library and seemed to go on forever. As he walked back to his second study, he told of how much he loved reading and showed off his private and signed collection of rare books. Rick says that he has read a book a day since he was fourteen years old.[3]

That's a lot of books! Reading is the key to unlocking wisdom and ability within yourself. You can read a thousand pages a day, but if you don't put those teachings into practice it becomes a wasted effort. My point is that it doesn't matter how much knowledge you accumulate if you don't put that knowledge into action. All the knowledge in the world means nothing without action. The secret combination is knowledge plus action. Knowledge and action have a linked and highly dependent relationship. They don't work well without each other. Learn to never use one without the other.

Sometimes things are out of your control; I'm not arguing that you have control at all times. But you can always control your reaction to those circumstances. Your reaction is something you can control every single time. You can either try and learn from your situation or you can ignore it and move on, only to possibly make the same mistake again and again. When you repeatedly make the same mistake, you are simply wasting time and most likely growing in frustration. Sometimes the stress we face in our lives is due in large part to the habits we create and not what's happening to us. I can't stress to you enough how important it is to never stop learning, from yourself and more importantly others. When you begin to realize the potential of this mindset switch, an exciting new world will open up for you. You will begin to see the potential of each day and view each moment as an opportunity.

There's so much to learn in this lifetime and there are so many new experiences and lessons to be had today. To some people, this can be overwhelming. They like being comfortable, and they know that when you grow, it's uncomfortable. Learning and growing can be very uncomfortable, but they can also be embraced. Learn to embrace the uncomfortable and set your mind on enjoying the tough seasons of life. Don't let the fact that you don't know everything be discouraging to you–let it be a motivation.

BE BETTER

I am a highly competitive person, and anyone that knows me probably thinks that's an understatement. It doesn't matter what I am doing, I want to win any game I play. In my mind, there's really no point in playing a game if you don't strive for victory. And winning is a lot more fun than losing. It could be a game of pickleball, a board game, or simply a made-up game of throwing rocks against a trash can. It doesn't matter - if I'm doing it, I want to do it well and try my best to win. I've learned there's nothing wrong with this attitude, but I have also learned over the years that there can be an unhealthy side to competitiveness. You can get so upset when you lose that you lose control of your emotions or even worse, damage relationships with the people you're competing with. I've had times where I'm playing a game of tennis, and I get so mad at myself for losing that I walk off without saying a word. Of course, I'm mad at myself for not playing well, but my silence speaks loudly.

I've had other times where I say too many words, and I speak negatively to myself or my friend I'm competing against. It's obviously never a good thing to throw a temper tantrum when you lose. What good does it do? You might temporarily release the built-up anger, but it's a short-term solution for a long-term problem. It's just a band-aid. I've been there before–thrown my racket and cursed out loud. It's just awkward for all those involved when you throw a temper tantrum over a bad shot or losing a game. I do hope and strive to never be there again, but it is very difficult when one is competitive.

Over the years, my competitive drive hasn't diminished. In fact, it's probably gotten stronger. But I've learned to harness that competitive drive into accelerated learning and hopefully helping others excel at whatever it is we are competing in. If I learn something that is helpful, I'm happy to share what I've discovered. And the biggest thing I've learned is that making your counterpart better will allow you to become better. It will strengthen your weaknesses and allow you to not put so much pressure on yourself. It will also allow you to have more fun in competition. Competition is meant to be competitive, not one-sided.

In recent years, I have actually learned to root for my opponent during play. I genuinely mean that, and there's good reason for it. I'm not necessarily rooting for them to win, but for them to compete and play at a high level. This doesn't mean I don't want to win or don't care, but the exact opposite. I want people around me to play at their best level, to elevate me to another level as well. It's a winning relationship. You can be highly competitive and still care for others in the process. It's definitely not one or the other.

In my experience, the best times in competition are when you are evenly matched with an opponent. You are pushing each other to make a better shot or execute a better move. You know that if you are off that day, your opponent will probably beat you. You have to focus. In order to win, you need to play your best, and therefore, your evenly matched opponent tends to bring the best out of you. The games are usually close and oftentimes they go into overtime or drain every ounce of physical and mental energy you have. Your opponent should be respected and revered, and she often is. She is playing a vital role in you becoming the best you can be.

Speaking of tennis, I remember watching the Roger Federer and Rafael Nadal rivalry. The two tennis stars would battle it out on the court, both physically and mentally. Some consider it to be the greatest rivalry in tennis history. The two stars were evenly matched, with both having their own strengths. Nadal preferred clay, while Federer preferred the hard court and grass. Federer was machine-like, while Nadal could chase down anything. Matches would seemingly last half the day. Sometimes Nadal would win, and sometimes Federer would win. It also stood out to me how much they respected one another's competitive drive and ability. It was another level of respect. Both men genuinely hated to lose, but when they did, they often spoke highly of the other person and were grateful to have competed against him. Nadal knew that playing Federer made him better. Federer knew that playing Nadal made him better. They were both fiercely competitive but at the same time fiercely grateful for one another.

The worst is when it's one-sided and one competitor demolishes the other time after time. The losing side loses motivation and the winning side gets complacent. This scenario is not helpful to either side. It only boosts the ego of the winner and demoralizes the loser. When two sides are equal in skill, it pushes each side to be better. When you root for your opponent to improve and play well, you improve yourself. As long as you're willing to work and learn, both sides can push each other to become better. This continues as far as both sides are willing to go.

I've seen this first hand since my days in middle school. I have two close friends with whom I have shared numerous competitive battles. We have played basketball, baseball, video games, darts, cards, and plenty of made-up games. We have shared profanity-laced tirades, physical fights, heated arguments, and massive successes (when we played on the same team). What I love most about our competitive relationship is that we made each other better. We fiercely competed, but at the end of the day, we were still friends. We would talk about strategies and techniques, which in turn made the other two better. If one of us became hands-down better at something, through hard work and knowledge, it would propel the other two to work harder or figure out how to compete. We all made each other better. Our wives may not understand our relationship to this day, but we do, and that's all that matters.

We still compete to this day and often do business together. We aren't as active as we once were, but the competitiveness is still there and has mostly transferred to business. We are all striving to be the best version of ourselves by collecting knowledge, wisdom, and widening our business intellect. When we learn something new and advantageous for ourselves, we pass that information along to the other two. There is no selfishness in wanting to keep it all to ourselves, but instead, we strive to make each other better–*better for our spouses, kids, friends, and family.* It creates a bond in trust and friendship that is not easily broken. We can still be highly competitive with one another, but we all know that at the end of the day, we are all in this life together and striving to be the best we can be for those around us. We share accomplishments and share in our struggles. The hard times make us better and the accomplishments give us a reason to celebrate. Having trusted friends or family around you as you grow is as vital to your growth as food is for your body. You don't want to go too long without it as it will greatly hinder your ability to function.

On the other hand, competition doesn't always go smoothly. Even when you have a growth mindset, you can still get upset with yourself or others. You can create triggers within the competition that lead to bad habits that, if not kept in check, can lead to more negative outcomes. One bad habit I got into early was using profanity when I competed. It started in high school during my baseball playing days. It became a way of releasing tension and frustration during the game or practice. It made me feel better as I was saying the words, but I felt like I had lost my control soon after. It became a habit. When I messed up a routine play, struck out, or even when an opponent scored a run, I would get frustrated. That frustration defaulted into a profanity-laced tirade. To say the least, it didn't help me. The profanity made me feel better for five seconds and then the words would sink in. There was a time that I could actually feel the weight of these words weighing me down during competition. I had called myself a f****** moron for messing up and soon realized that I had hurt my own feelings. It's laughable now, but it made me stop and realize that words carry meaning, especially words spoken to yourself.

If the goal is to encourage and build up, speaking words of negativity do not help in any way. It has been said many ways, but Lisa Hayes once said, *"Be careful how you are talking to yourself because you are listening."*[4] That is such an undervalued quote for most of the people in this world. If you don't believe in yourself, who will? If you don't see the positive aspects of learning from failures, who will? It's something to ponder and think about the next time you get frustrated in an activity, sport, or job. How you respond to yourself is vital in your path to becoming a better version of yourself.

Once I realized how harmful speaking down to myself could be, I needed to do something different going forward. As an alternative to degrading myself, I started repeating the words, *"be better,"* to my inner self. I know my inner warrior is always listening, and ripe for encouragement. Most people will never hear the encouragement I speak to myself, but it doesn't matter. What matters is that I hear it. This simple pivot in reaction shifted my mindset in an impactful way. I began seeing poor shots or mess-ups as lessons learned and began trying to dissect them in my mind. This not only allowed me to rapidly improve in new areas but also gave me an appreciation for the great shots my opponent made against me.

Sometimes, people just make a good shot or a great decision in life. It shouldn't be demeaning to you and it doesn't have to be a comparison to your ability. It's simply a well-executed shot in gameplay or a great decision in life. Learn to appreciate it and grow from it.

When someone does make a perfect shot or gets that job promotion you should have received, it can still be frustrating. You think to yourself, "That should have been me", or think, "That was just lucky." But was it lucky? Or is this a situation where your skill level is not where it needs to be? Asking yourself, "Why?" is a great starting point. Try to come back to the mindset of learning from each and every situation or play.

There are times when your athletic ability isn't at the level where you can make the shot you want, and you may not have the wisdom to make that key business decision. But you can get there. The first step is fully believing you can get there. The shots you see professionals make are misleading; they seem effortless. It seems that way because they've devoted so much time to improving and becoming the best they can be. They may know something or have skills that you don't yet have. Open your mind to learn and grow. Seek mentors and learn from others. Make mistakes. Lean into those mistakes and realize they are there for a reason. Become better in the future by consciously learning from the present.

The Main Ingredients

.

Chapter Two

HUMILITY
IS GOLD

"On the highest throne in the world,
we still sit only on our own bottom."

– Michel de Montaigne

Why is humility such a crucial ingredient in your growth and development? Because it puts you in a frame of mind to prepare to learn. If you're not practicing humility, you may act like you know everything or think that your way is best. No discussions, no asking questions, it's just your way or the highway. With a know-it-all mindset, why would you ever listen to the advice of others? They're always wrong, and you're always right. Your growth is suspended. This unfortunately is what happens all too often when people enter adulthood. They lose their humility. They lose the ability to understand that no one has all the answers. There might be pressure from their children or apprentices to seem like they know it all, but no one can live up to that. No one will ever know all there is to know. We just don't have enough time or mental capacity. The truth is this: you don't know everything. You need to start acting like it!

When a person is humble, it's like having the master key to a multitude of doors to your future. There are multiple options for you to explore along the way. Staying in this frame of mind is very difficult and that's why so few do it. But the ones that can stay humble are primed to grow exponentially. Those humble pioneers are able to listen, respond, and act in a positive way. They create opportunities through putting aside their egos and simply learning something they don't know. When you live in humility, doors will inevitably open.

One of my favorite lessons in the Bible is from Ecclesiastes. It paints a picture of why humility is so important for leaders to possess.

"There was a small city with few men. A mighty king came against

it, surrounded it, and built large siege ramps against it. Now a poor wise man was found in the city, and he saved the city by his wisdom. Yet no one remembered that poor man. And I said, 'Wisdom is better than strength, but the wisdom of the poor man is despised, and his words are not heeded.'" (Ecclesiastes 9:14)[5]

There are many different takeaways from this verse and maybe that's why it means so much to me. The biggest takeaway for me is that you can learn from anyone. It doesn't matter how successful, how dumb, or how poor he might sound when he talks. There is untapped potential and wisdom from everyone around you, whether they be poor or wealthy. It could be hidden in an aging employee in your business, a random stranger at a coffee shop, or your crazy uncle that you try to avoid at family gatherings. The key to discovering this potential is humility. Have the humility to ask questions or just simply listen, no matter who you're asking the question to.

HIDDEN VALUE

Every single person in this world has value, and everyone has valuable life experiences that can be shared if we choose to listen. Where does that value ultimately come from? I would confidently say it comes from God. No one else can give that value or take it away. If we work to stay in a humble frame of mind, knowing that God is the one that gave us life and it wasn't some chance encounter with the universe, it opens the door to so many more lessons and opportunities for growth, no matter the source. You can learn to see value and seek to learn from people who may seem incapable of possessing an ounce of wisdom. Truth and wisdom sometimes show up in the most obscure places. Learn to look for wisdom in unexpected situations.

I remember several conversations with people on many travels with my wife Kendra. Even though we had a guidebook and knew where we were going, sometimes we would stop to ask for directions. We did this to learn more about the area. People would share tips on what to see and what to avoid. People would tell us where to eat and what to do. Something I've learned is that no matter what city or town you're in, people are generally proud to live there. They are there for a reason and have years of experience living there. It might seem like a small thing to do, but asking a simple question about someone's hometown can open up a conversation and a point of view that many people don't get the opportunity to hear. Next time you're traveling, try starting a conversation with an employee at a coffee shop or a person sitting on a park bench. You'll never know what kind of useful information people are willing to share unless you are humble enough to ask.

While asking questions and listening, something very important to consider is filtering what people say. Not everything that comes out of people's mouths has value. Sometimes it's just gibberish, but as we grow in discernment and wisdom, we can filter through the seemingly invaluable jargon and find important takeaways. It's like an intellectual treasure hunt, full of clues and dead ends! Be willing to play the game and develop the skill of listening and discernment. Soon you'll find that simply allowing other people to be heard will not only allow you to grow, but it will give the person speaking a feeling of value. You don't have to agree with everything that person is saying, but it's almost always worth listening. It's one of the greatest win-win situations out there. You gain valuable insight and wisdom, and your counterpart feels good about themselves for sharing and helping you.

THE IMPORTANCE OF HUMILITY

Humility is not just a passive term that others use to keep you in line. It goes much deeper than the surface. It has massive spiritual meaning as well. When you walk in humility, the world opens up to you. You don't have to go around thinking less of yourself, but you do have to realize that you don't know everything. There is a relational abundance in not knowing everything. It allows us to connect with people that we might not normally connect with. Beyond the possible relationships, humility allows us to see the world as a child. Children are always seeking answers to simple questions, always improving, and always on the brink of learning something new. A child asks why they have to eat vegetables instead of candy, and why the grass is wet in the morning. Children tend to experience new feelings and physical experiences daily. Children don't take these experiences for granted like adults tend to. They relish in learning and take every chance to improve their physical and mental capacity. At some point, when we leave childhood, we become embarrassed to ask questions for fear of looking unintelligent. We are fearful of what others may think of us. Why has it taken us so long to learn something so simple? Others' perceptions of us can greatly inhibit our ability to learn and grow. If we didn't care what other people thought about our current state of intelligence, how much more could we learn? How much do you hold back knowing that someone could poke fun at you for not knowing the answer or understanding how to complete a task? We all miss opportunities all too often, myself included, for fear of what others may think.

According to Anthony Moore, being afraid of asking questions is the number one killer of dreams. In an article written by Moore titled How "to Stop Being Afraid of Looking Stupid" he tells the story of a little boy that witnesses the "cool" kid gracefully jumping from rock to rock in the schoolyard. The little boy, Moore's close friend, decided to try this for himself. He jumped, slipped, and fell hard to the dirt. With dirt on his pants and the heavy weight of embarrassment bearing down on him, he endured the cold laughter of his classmates. Those around him witnessed the outcome and probably dared not to try for fear of the same result. The little boy was ashamed of his efforts. To this day, Moore's friend is deathly afraid of trying anything new, for fear of failure.[6] That is all too common for most people. They feel the pain of failure and associate trying anything new with that pain. Trying something that you've never done before is not easy, but it doesn't have to be painful for you or those around you.

I would take Moore's article a step further and say that it's not only your dreams you kill, but you can easily murder the dreams of others with fear as well. Fear is a vicious weapon and a terrible mindset to pass along to friends or family. It's more contagious than any virus and is almost instantaneous. Fear isn't a skill that has to be worked on, it simply arrives uninvited and unannounced. It brings no value and takes value from all involved. When you experience fear, as we all do, try not to pass it along. Absorb it through prayer, meditation, or action. The less fear you can spread to others, the better your life and opportunities will be.

What if we worked through another outcome in the schoolyard? Instead of the "cool" kid acting better than everyone else and lording over the pawns, what if he reacted differently and paved the way for a new thought process? When Moore's friend fell, what if the "cool" kid helped him up and offered to teach him how to do it? He could have said, "It's okay–I did the same thing when I tried the first time, too." One act of humility and thirty seconds of encouragement could have redirected one life, if not many more witnessing the event that day. You see, humility works on both sides. It encourages and lifts both parties and can be applied to many areas of life. Humility is a wonder drug of immeasurable purpose. I don't say this lightly and honestly, I shy away from saying it under normal circumstances, but humility really could change the world, and it begins with you.

INTELLECTUAL HUMILITY

As a society, we desperately need intellectual humility. We all need to understand that we don't know everything and never will. No one has all the answers, and that's why questions and truthful answers to those questions are so important. Like we mentioned earlier, you can give value to others by allowing them to share the knowledge they possess. This can lead to them being heard and give you the opportunity to learn something new. When a person can fully engage in intellectual humility, she then has the ability to see people in a new way. She doesn't look down on others for not having specific knowledge, but instead looks to the side and realizes we are all in this together.

Every person has an abundance of knowledge in some area, even when that person considers themselves unintelligent. If you compare a farmer to a Wall Street trader, who would most of the world say is more intelligent? Most likely people would say the Wall Street trader with the Ivy League business degree. He makes more money and wears nice suits. But what if Wall Street was gone and that trader needed to grow his own food? That farmer now becomes the most intelligent person in the room. It's all in how you view the situation. There's nothing wrong with being a Wall Street trader, and there's nothing wrong with being a farmer. Could the farmer become a Wall Street trader? With the right mindset and mentors, yes. Could the trader become a farmer? Again, yes. Both have their own unique skill sets and vat of knowledge. They are wise and valuable in two different ways, but are also equal in value.

I believe the power of humility allows a person to see that we are all made from the same canvas. We all have potential. What we place on our canvas makes us who we are. Who we interact with and what we learn allows us to paint our own scene. We are constantly putting on new paint layers and adding to it until the day we die. When you stop painting, I believe you stop living. Your canvas doesn't have to be perfect. And there are so many ways to fill your canvas, such as pencil, watercolor, charcoal, or oil. It doesn't matter what medium you use, it only matters that you add layers. Don't be afraid to make your life an abstract masterpiece.

THE TRICK OF ADMITTING IGNORANCE

A funny thing happens when you admit that you don't know something. People will most likely try teaching you what you don't know. They don't feel intimidated, and they tend to share information freely and without fear of being criticized. Learn to listen in these moments, even if you know the answers. You want people you're interacting with in this frame of mind. When people are relaxed in any environment, they are more willing to share information and more likely to connect with others on a deeper level. You never know what you might learn from someone with experience, even if you have more experience yourself.

You've also probably heard the phrase, "Fake it 'til you make it." If not, I'm sure you'll come across it in any field or subject you're involved with at some point. I used to believe that was the best way to go about your business and even life. If you don't know how to do something, just take the job, act like you do, and then get it done. However, I found there's a much better way. What you sacrifice in the short term, you gain in the long term, and what you gain in the short term, you sacrifice in the long term. Let me explain further. If you act as you know it all, you will rarely be taught new things. Your learning curve will be slow and stunted. The opportunities you have for growth will be few and far between. People may think you have it all together, but you can only fake it for so long. You tend to fill in the gaps with your own dead-end thoughts and even lies. Sooner or later, you will need to become a resource and not just a deflector. People will eventually see through this, and it's not a very good long-term plan.

Instead of faking it, own your ignorance and inability. I mean really own it. Like I mentioned earlier, there can even be times when asking someone to explain something that you're well versed in can be a great learning experience. You may know ten things about a certain process or subject, but there could be a hidden eleventh step that you're not aware of. When you ask, you allow other people to show their value. I've said it before, but it's important to understand: when someone teaches you something, it adds value to both you and them. It's the best win-win there is in my opinion.

When people feel valued, productivity increases, relationships strengthen, and more opportunities will be available for both parties. When you give value to another person, they're more willing to engage you in conversation again because you lifted them up by asking and listening. You don't have to speak words of encouragement to lift someone's spirits. Sometimes all you have to do is ask and listen.

Can it be embarrassing for you to admit you don't know something? It obviously can be, but it can also be liberating. When you approach a conversation from a place of humility, you open the door for real conversation and growth. That authenticness is what you're searching for. Would you rather be embarrassed in the short term or disappointed at the end of your life looking back at what you could have done differently? I would gladly take the short-term embarrassment and learn how to handle my emotions. I can personally attest that learning to embrace temporary embarrassment will lead to much growth and prosperity.

In the end, the more you fake it, the more opportunities for authenticity and growth you miss out on. The less you fake it and lean into learning, the better your conversations, and the faster your growth can be. Learn to admit when you don't know something and see where it leads you. If you're up for the challenge, there's a lot of green grass on the other side of embarrassment and admitting ignorance.

Chapter Three

CURIOSITY IS KEY

"I have no special talent. I am only
passionately curious."

- Albert Einstein

Leaders and learners do not need to know everything. They never do, and they never will. When people try to tell themselves that they have all the answers, it usually ends badly for them and those around them. They act like they don't need help from anyone, and when they actually do need help, they often won't admit it. They are stuck in a constant battle of trying to keep their superior image. Trying to keep up with a false image doesn't tend to end well for most people.

However, there is a simple solution. After embracing humility, one of the key skills that leaders need more than anything is curiosity. Yes, curiosity is a major skill, not just a fleeting feeling for cats. It is something you can develop and build upon. Being curious allows you to continually expand your wealth of knowledge and internal database. Curiosity can be applied to anything: people, places, things–it doesn't matter. As you learn to harness the power of curiosity and stay in a humble frame of mind, you'll find that people and places can come alive. Dull moments become opportunities to explore, and people you thought weren't worth your time become unforgettable.

Having a genuine curiosity helps you pay attention in a conversation that you would normally have little interest in. If you're curious about the people in the conversation, you're more likely to be willing to listen and comprehend what is being said. You want to learn more about them because you're highly curious about their story. What brought them to the point they're at now? What motivates them, and what's the reason they get out of bed in the morning? Being curious also helps you stay in the present moment. It will add value to your conversations and people will notice.

When you are genuinely curious about someone or something, your questions become more thoughtful. You become more intentional and interactive. People will really notice the difference. And you can't fake curiosity. Curiosity comes out through not just your words, but your body language as well. Try to fake being curious and see what happens. If people are paying attention to you, they can tell you are disengaged or your mind is elsewhere. If your mind wanders, your body will soon follow.

You can and should be curious about the past or future, but the present is where you learn, grow, and show respect to those around you. You are either curious or you're not, there's no in-between. You can't be half curious, just like you can't halfway focus. Start building the skill of curiosity and see where it leads. If you're one for adventure, there's plenty of adventures and conversations that come with being curious.

Just like anything, curiosity is not always the best answer for all situations. After all, curiosity did kill the cat *(supposedly)*. If you're in a situation where you are curious about a button on a battleship, you probably shouldn't push it to see what happens. Instead, you can ask questions, not take immediate action.

Curiosity needs to be developed and refined, just like any other skill. An out-of-control curiosity can lead you to some pretty terrible outcomes. While I believe it's highly important to be curious, it's also very important to be curious within the rules of morality.

DEVELOPING YOUR CURIOSITY

How does one develop curiosity? Being open to new ideas and ways of doing things is a great start. Just because you have a certain way of doing things, doesn't mean there's not another way. There may even be a better way you're just currently unaware of. It also doesn't mean that the way you're doing it now is incorrect. You could learn that your old way is the best, but if you don't experiment with processes, you'll never know.

Keep an open mind, being ready to test your skills at any given time. People tend to get comfortable with their habits and are often intimidated by change. Learn to appreciate potential change and do your best to look for it. Change happens all the time, but you want to make change happen on purpose.

People often overestimate the amount of time it takes to learn something new and create a new habit or way of thinking. They overcomplicate and overestimate what it takes to bring change. It could take only a few minutes to learn something new and apply it to your life. The refusal to even try is where people get it wrong. Getting started is over half the battle, but once you start, it can have a dramatic snowball effect. Tasks you once thought were hard no longer seem hard, and situations you used to be afraid of are not so scary anymore.

Asking questions and learning to keep quiet is another great way of forming your curiosity skill. When you ask a question and let someone else speak, you will be amazed at what you will learn when you pay attention. Not every conversation will be worth getting into again, but learning to love and value silence on your end and letting other people speak opens up information that most people don't normally share. Start by asking a friend a question. Let her answer, and then follow her answer with, "tell me more," or "and why is that?" Then be quiet and let her continue. See how far she will take you into her story. If her first answer is only chapter one in her story, make it a game to find out how many total chapters she has in her book.

Awkward silence is also a great tool. Most people don't like silence and they will start speaking just to fill the air. Learn to love the silence of the in-between. Be aware of body language and what is happening without any verbal dialogue. Everyone is unique and has a different story that can be told with or without words. If you enjoy reading books or watching movies, then having a good conversation with someone should be a priority and enjoyment as well. Learn to see the story in individuals and value it. And just because you listen to someone's story doesn't mean you have to agree with him. Listening does not equal agreement. That's important to understand. It allows you to fully listen and not interrupt after every point of disagreement. It's tough and most people can't handle it, but great people can.

Trying new things on purpose is a great test of how curious (and patient) you currently are. If you purposefully get out of a habit or routine, you are fully conscious of your forgoing actions and ready to see things from a different perspective. You can start small by walking a new path in your neighborhood or trying to fix that vegetable you hate in a new, hopefully delicious, way. You will start to see things in a fresh way and not just be on autopilot. The human mind is a beautiful creation, but it can prevent you from seeing new perspectives. To consolidate energy, your brain will put your mind on autopilot and place everyday actions in the back of your mind.[7] This action is a great efficiency for our mind, but it can be a hindrance. Learn to be aware of this and when the situation calls for a new perspective, step out from your autopilot mode.

Once you get comfortable with trying small things, branch out and try something completely new, like building a piece of furniture or attending a cooking workshop. Hone your curiosity into something that propels you forward and allows your mind to open to new possibilities. Trying new things and stepping out of your comfort zone can become fun and exhilarating.

To reiterate, I believe that the key to curiosity is nothing other than humility. When a person is humble, she isn't trying to be right, she is trying to learn. That person knows that when she interacts with a person or subject, she doesn't know everything. This is a powerful frame of mind, and it's not easy, but it's the key to fully developing your own curiosity.

Without humility, curiosity will become questionable and counterfeit, like you're just trying to take something that isn't yours. You'll engage to draw the life out of people for your own gain. Without humility, curiosity can be selfish. Learn to ask questions in humility in order to learn together when the opportunity is present. Learn to be humble in private and more importantly in public. Without humility, curiosity dies a quick death.

Remember, curiosity does take a large amount of energy and

brainpower. When you're engaged in a good conversation, have you noticed how you get tired and feel like your energy has been drained from you? It might not be for the reasons you believe. It's because you were focused and worked your brain intellectually and emotionally. People often think the only way to be tired is to be physically tired, but that's not true. You can drain yourself just by talking and engaging in conversations all day long.

Ask a psychologist. I'm sure they will tell you that engaging with patients all day long is exhausting. Doctors can't just routinely shut off their brains and coast through a vital conversation with a patient, as they are forced to stay engaged. Ask a parent. Parents will tell you that hearing their kids ask for things or complain all day is tiresome.

Just as you can train your body to be in better physical shape, you can train your mind to handle a larger intake of conversations. You can train your brain to be more emotionally and intellectually fit. Start small and work your way up. Start paying attention and engaging in small chunks of time. Build your focus muscle and begin engaging for longer periods of time.

You don't go out and run a marathon from day one, so don't be discouraged if you're tired after one short conversation. As funny as it sounds, people can be worn out from short conversations. That's why some people you meet don't enjoy conversation, because it literally wears them out. Stay focused and build your curiosity muscle. The more you embrace being consciously curious, the faster the world will open up to you.

Chapter Four

THE FALLACY OF SELF-MADE

"If I have seen further than others, it is by standing upon the shoulders of giants."

- Sir Isaac Newton

I hear it all the time. It shows up in the news, magazine articles, and everyday conversations. The pundits proclaim that he is a self-made millionaire! And that she made all her money on her own. But it couldn't be further from the truth! There is no such thing as "self-made" anything. I don't care who says it, they're wrong, or they don't fully understand what they're actually saying. Every single person, no matter how successful, is made from people that have poured skill and know-how into their lives.

Parents or grandparents that taught them invaluable lessons when they were young that helped shape habits and mindset. People that dedicated time, money, and wisdom into books, on-line seminars, or in person meetings. If people believe they're self-made, they're often overlooking those who have had an impact on their lives. That person isn't giving credit where credit is due. Even if the self-made guru came from nothing and had an extraordinarily hard path, he didn't invent every little thing that has empowered him to succeed in life. It might be a great accomplishment, but there are so many people to credit and be thankful for along the way.

Let's break it down to the basics. From the moment you wake up, you get out of a warm bed you didn't create, grab coffee beans that you didn't harvest, and pour the coffee into a cup that you didn't design. You then grab your smart phone, get into your car, and drive on a road that you didn't pave. You drive into a city you had no part in starting and sit down at a computer that you had no part in inventing. I could go on and on, but you get my point. There is obviously nothing wrong with using everyday items that you had no part in making, but the point is that you are where you are with the help of people from the past. There are numerous everyday items we take for granted that help propel us on to new levels of success. You may be a part of future inventions, but even those future ideas depend in large part on the available resources you have today. Those resources are provided to you by hard working people that have come before you.

Sir Isaac Newton said, *"If I have seen further, it is by standing on the shoulders of giants."*[8] One of the brightest minds of the 17th century was able to see past his own brilliance and say with humility that he owed his success to those that had come before him. It takes a humble person to become wise. The more wisdom you accumulate, the more you often realize you don't know. Newton was known to be a very wise individual. He knew that everything he had accomplished and would accomplish in the future was directly related to those who had done the work before him. These people paved the way for his success. His predecessors gave him the platform and foundation to think at a higher level. He was grateful and humble, and it allowed him to elevate beyond what he ever could on his own.

No one is self-made, it's simply not possible. The next time someone says they are "self-made", I encourage you to ask him some simple questions. How did you learn what you know? How many mistakes did you bypass by taking someone else's advice? Start a conversation, but don't be condescending and threatening. If they don't understand what you are referring to or they get upset, just move on to another topic. People tend to see what they want to see and until they're ready, it's not usually worth an argument.

This concept of gratitude, rooted in humility, is vitally important to recognize. You cannot do life alone, it's simply not possible. Let me reiterate. You cannot do life without people teaching and guiding you. People can and will be present in your life in many ways, not just in person. Be humble enough to admit this and wise enough to recognize the people that have invested time and wisdom into your life. You may be able to become successful, due to your own ambition, but you learn and grow from other people paving your path.

We only have a limited number of years, days, and breaths. Don't waste them by speaking about yourself and your great accomplishments. Your accomplishments can and should be shared, but they can also speak for themselves. Use your time and energy to speak life and blessings into others. Understand the magnitude of sacrifice and hard work that others have made so that you may have a chance to succeed. Don't waste time trying to figure everything out on your own and thinking that it's you against the world. It's a lonely path, and you'll be the only one waiting to congratulate yourself at the end.

A FOUNDATION FOR YOUR SUCCESS

Have you ever stopped to think about all the pieces that have been put in place for you to have a chance at success? No matter what you do or aspire to do, someone has gone before you and paved the way for you to succeed. Even if not directly related to you, they have provided better odds for your success. It doesn't matter what it is! Like we discussed previously, think about every advantage you currently have that you can easily overlook. Not just your parents' sacrifices, but the country to which you were born, the year you arrived, and the people you will never meet that established the foundation for you to be great. Be grateful for those sacrifices and advantages and use them as a tool for your humility and future gains.

Last week, I was driving with my wife on our way to a new investment property and started thinking to myself: *"Someone has paid for and done all the work to pave this road that leads to our real estate. Without the road, the house would not be accessible. On top of that, the electric company has already run electricity to our area. There is a man-made lake, which our house overlooks, and a boat dock, ready to go. The foundation is there for us to succeed in our endeavors. If we were to try and do everything by ourselves, there would be a lot of work that needed to be done before our chance at success would be anywhere near what it is today. It may take decades instead of months. I am so thankful for those who have sacrificed, built, and envisioned the building blocks that we enjoy today."*

Think through a situation in your life that is similar. From the moment you entered the picture, what foundation was laid before you arrived? Think of all the ways your predecessors sacrificed and provided you the opportunity to succeed. It could be a promotion at your job, a painting masterpiece you created, or success on the sports field. Remember the connections that led you to get your job, or the canvas and paints that someone else created to allow you to paint, or the random game that some creative person invented years ago that you now get the opportunity to enjoy. The more you remember and the more you are grateful for, the better your life and the lives of those around you will be.

SIDE-STEPPING ARROGANCE

I don't feel the need to beat this point into the ground, but I do think it's important to understand the advantages of being grateful to those that have come before you.

First of all, when you're grateful to other people, you tend to treat them differently. You assign to them value and that received value can give them meaning and lift their spirits. When you value people, you don't simply use them and then discard them out for your own personal gain. Gratefulness allows you to see people and situations from a different perspective. This unique perspective often gives meaning to overlooked historic events and the sacrifices generations before us have made.

Secondly, when you acknowledge everyone that's come before you and graciously (or not so graciously) given you the opportunity to succeed, you give yourself the ability to side-step being arrogant. Arrogance is a dark trait that I would recommend to avoid. Too many people suffer from this selfish and idol-like way to carry themselves. It may seem like society rewards those arrogant know-it-alls, but I'm going to tell you that it doesn't work out in the end. Gratefulness is the medicine to the sickness of arrogance.

While an arrogant person tries to prove their dominance or show power over another individual, a grateful person empowers their peers. When arrogance tells you to take all the credit, gratefulness acknowledges your partner's sacrifices.

You may be self-motivated or prefer to work alone, but those are two entirely different things. Learn to be grateful for the people you know and don't know that have paved the way for your success. Those people didn't guarantee your success, but they did guarantee the opportunity for success that you currently have. The sooner you realize that you are not self-made, the better off you'll be.

Chapter Five

THE LOST ART
OF MENTORSHIP

"Mentoring is a brain to pick, an ear to
listen, and a push in the right direction."

- John C. Crosby

When you think of a mentor, who comes to mind? Does your father or mother take that role, or is it a coach or family friend? Whoever it is, hopefully, they made a positive and lasting impact on the trajectory of your life. Or even better, hopefully, they are still pouring wisdom into your life today! Without numerous mentors during my early years, and even still to this day, my life would look completely different. There's no doubt that I would not be on the same path I'm on now without these invaluable mentors. The wisdom, small tips, and life hacks they taught me when I was young allowed me to skip mistakes and grow as a person at a greater pace. But it only worked if I listened to what they were teaching. I've had people give me great advice in the past that I did not listen to. As a consequence, I had to experience that failure myself later on. That extra step could have been avoided if I had only taken their advice to heart.

We can learn from anyone, but observation is the first step. Observing can be listening or simply watching. Putting those wise lessons into action is the next step. Without listening and observing, there can be no learning. Without action, observing doesn't matter. You have to combine both of these skills in order to move forward. If you can master the art of observation, your available mentors will double, triple, or even quadruple overnight.

Trusting who your mentor is and what they are teaching is highly important as well. If there is no trust, there can be no vulnerability, and learning is significantly more difficult. The close mentors you learn from don't have to be perfect, but they do need to have your best interest in mind. If they are selfish and tend to use you for their own gain, the trust will be lacking. If you can't trust these people, then you have to work extremely hard to filter what they are teaching you. You have to take the time and energy to make sure what they are teaching you is correct and not just for their gain. Finding trustworthy mentors is a critical component of your success. Find people that will selflessly help you grow and celebrate your successes along the way. You will be better for it and your mentor will be better for it as well.

It seems that the more "intelligent" we become as a society, fewer and fewer people think they need mentors. They have this smart device in their pocket that is always available with any answer they need. Why ask another person for advice when you have all you need in your pocket? Why even pay attention to another person when they are talking? Technology is a gift, but when it hinders your ability to grow and connect with people, it's a nuisance, not a tool. Reliance on your phone instead of storing wisdom in your mind is not growth, it's dependence. You don't want to depend on a device that you could misplace or break on any given day. Beyond getting past the dependence on technology, the interaction with a mentor is what's important and sorely needed. The ability to ask a question in the middle of a stressful situation or the timely feedback of a job well done is what's important. The real-time correction of a good mentor allows us to learn well. Feedback when we do something right, and feedback when we do something wrong, is vital. Technology can't give us this and no matter how much it promises, it will never take the place of a real-world mentor.

Maybe people just often overlook a potential mentor and they don't realize what is actually taking place. People become so self-obsessed with their accomplishments and think they did everything on their own. Worse yet, they think they can do everything on their own and don't need anything more. They don't need anyone telling them what to do or correcting their missteps. This way of thinking only prevents growth and meaningful relationships. A great mentoring relationship will allow you to skip ahead and learn from the mistakes of your mentor. You don't have to live it to learn from it. It's a cheat code that's not cheating. It's intelligence and humility at their finest.

MEANINGFUL MENTORSHIP

Do you know where the word mentor originated? The English word "mentor" was taken from the writings of Homer's epic *The Odyssey*. When Odysseus was away from home, the son he left as a baby, Telemachus, grew up under the supervision of a man named Mentor. Mentor was known as an old, trusted friend. Athena even thought so highly of Mentor that she disguised herself as Mentor in the story to gain Telemachus' trust.[9] The concept of a mentor may have been put into writing by Homer, but the process has been around since the beginning of time. Today, the word "mentor" is used for anyone who has a positive and guiding influence on another person's life.[10]

Great mentor/mentee relationships in the past include Socrates, who mentored Plato, and then Plato began mentoring Aristotle, who then went on to mentor Alexander the Great. Henry David Thoreau mentored Ralph Waldo Emerson. Tiger Woods was mentored by his father, Earl Woods. Audrey Hepburn mentored Elizabeth Taylor. This list is endless, and such great examples continue throughout generations. And it doesn't have to be grand examples of famous people! Oprah was said to be mentored by her elementary school teacher. You could be mentored by a family member or close friend. Your parents or grandparents could be your greatest mentors. A mentor needs to be able to push you into new ways of thinking and involve you in the learning process. Reciprocal trust is the most important aspect. The mentee must fully trust the mentor's wisdom, and the mentor must trust the mentee to follow through with the advice. Without that trust, it's impossible to grow beyond the surface of the relationship.

Another matter to ponder is the amount of mentors you're able to include in your life. The average millionaire has seven streams of income. These income streams protect your wealth and lifestyle against times when a job is lost or an investment goes bad. Relating this to mentorship, I believe every person should have an average of seven mentors in his/her life. If one mentor is lost or another decides to move on, you still have six other guides to help you stay on the right path. You are not confined to just one mentor, and honestly you're better off having multiple people you can learn and gain insight from.

With multiple mentors in your life, one can teach you about money, and another mentor can teach you morals. One friend can teach you how to shoot a basketball, and another friend can show you how to treat others with kindness. It's important to remember that no one does everything right or has all the answers. Just because one mentor is great in one area doesn't mean they excel in all areas. Having multiple mentors in your life will give you the greatest chance at being the best you can be.

FRIENDS AND MENTORS

When I think back to all the mentors I've had growing up, it honestly brings tears to my eyes. I imagine myself standing atop a stone castle with everyone who has had an impact in my life. These amazing people form the foundation of my castle. The height of the castle grows with new mentors and wisdom, and allows me to see further and further. The incredible view is even more stunning the higher my castle rises into the air. The best part is enjoying the view with everyone who has taught and encouraged me along the way!

My first and most important mentors were my parents. They allowed me to ask them questions, make mistakes, and helped encourage me in the right direction. My dad was tough when he needed to be tough and understanding when I needed grace. I honestly believe that I had one of the best dads who has ever lived. He wasn't perfect, but he helped mold me into a man. My mom also played a significant role in my growth. She was tough on me when I needed it and gentle when I needed someone to listen. She's not a perfect person either, but I feel like she was the perfect mother. The two of them combined to be the best parents and mentors I could ask for. I still consider my parents mentors to this day and will still seek advice with tough questions and situations. They don't always have the answer, but that's not what matters. What matters is how they shape my thought process and the fact that they have always been there when I have needed them. Without my parents forming the base of my mentorship castle, I know I would not be where I am today.

To say I lucked out with in-laws is an understatement. From my second mom and dad, I've learned a great deal on faith, family, and quality time, over the short years I've been around. The humility and spiritual intelligence my second set of parents possess is phenomenal. I could go on and on about them, but they really are special and I couldn't imagine my life at this point without them either.

I have always looked up to my grandparents as mentors, as well. Both sets of my grandparents were dairy farmers and taught me hard work through actions, not words. My mother's father, Ferguson, had a big impact on my life, in part because I was so close in proximity to him. I grew up across the street from their house and began working on the farm at a young age. From feeding calves to scraping cow manure off stalls, anytime I had a question, he would be there to answer that question or be willing to talk through it. He was always very gentle and never condemning, although there were times when he knew the work just needed to be done. Nothing fancy, just good old-fashioned work. No excuses, just get it done. He didn't have a college education, but he was one of the wisest men I've ever known. He knew more about plants and animals *(without having to ask a search engine)* than most people can fathom. He was constantly working on the farm, but somehow found time to talk to anyone and everyone. He was greatly loved for that. He wasn't perfect but he was a great man. He showed by example how to be a hard-working individual and still value people. He also wasn't afraid to teach others what he knew. He wanted the best for them, so he listened and mentored anyone that made the time.

From Lowell, my dad's father, I witnessed the power of a good story, and how that story can be elevated when told around a crisp, fall campfire. I always loved to hear my grandpa laugh and learned that laughter is an essential nutrient to the soul. Both of my grandfathers have passed away and I miss both of them dearly. The love and wisdom they shared with me will never be forgotten. I still see parts of them in conversations with other wise men from the greatest generation the world has ever seen. I know that's why I try my best to stop and listen anytime I come across an older and wiser man looking for a conversation. I look forward to seeing them both again one day soon.

Other mentors in my life include my aunt and uncle who ran a carpet cleaning business. I worked for them growing up as well, and I picked up many lessons along the way. My uncle knows more about carpets, how to clean them, and how to preserve rare oriental rugs than anyone in the country. That's not an exaggeration. My aunt is amazing with people, very knowledgeable, and keeps everything behind the scenes running smoothly. They are both amazing in their own right but need each other. I worked for them early on and learned how a great partnership really works. Strong on their own, but so much better together. Again, they aren't perfect, but I still talk with them to this day and consider them mentors. I learned that through other people's imperfections, perfect partnerships can be formed. Partnerships require different skills. Without imperfections, partners aren't needed.

One of my mom's brothers still runs the farm to this day. He lived as a single dad for years, while raising kids and running a farm. He's not perfect, but he's an inspiration to me. A great example of why I look up to him happened recently. I had managed to get a twenty-six foot U-Haul truck stuck in my backyard and I was not in a good mood. He had a tractor, and I knew he could help me out, so I called him for a favor. He stopped what he was doing and came to help. After assessing the situation, he and his son pulled the truck out with ease. Expecting to get made fun of when I walked up to thank him (and it was well deserved), he simply said, *"Now, what did you learn?"* Taken back, I had no idea what I learned and didn't really know what to say, but he proceeded to tell me what happened. He said to never run a truck near a septic tank, as there is always soft mud, even many years after it has been installed. He just smiled, hopped on his red tractor, and went about his day. Uncle Jordon to the rescue and a valuable lesson learned. There's almost always a lesson hidden somewhere in my many failings if I'm willing to set aside my ego and listen with humility.

I have another uncle who sells handmade, antique lures. He and his wife have one of the best examples of a loving marriage that I've been around. My uncle Kevin owns his own propane company, and he and his wife Debbie are always a joy and a blast to be around. My dad's brother started his own radio show many years back. My dad's cousin is a high-ranking officer in the army. I have cousins that run a food truck and other family members that I pick up little things here and there from, even if I only have a chance to see them once a year.

My wife has a gigantic family where dreamers and entrepreneurial minds abound. Family get-togethers are always fascinating. There is really no limit to what I have access to and what I can learn if I just pay attention. There's no one that I'm purposefully not paying attention to. Everyone has value, you just have to be willing to look for it.

I have many mentors outside of my family as well. My wife and I had the amazing opportunity and pleasure of meeting Jon and Josh Bailey early in our entrepreneurial careers. They started a company with their longtime friend David Yount called Lightstock. When Kendra and I were first venturing out into self-employment, we were looking for opportunities to provide steady income for the business. We divinely stumbled upon Lightstock, and I called Josh right away to ask more information on the company. His tone and readiness to help was energizing. We began as a photography partners with Lightstock almost immediately and soon visited the Lightstock team in Texas. From our first meeting, it was clear that we wanted to be around them and learn all we could from their motivational and friendly business style. These three mentors met every challenge with determination and grace. They led their team with a loving understanding that few leaders possess. They have vision and drive. Jon, Josh, and David have since started the bible reading app Dwell. A massive undertaking, we watched them hit every milestone with Dwell, and they continue (to this day) to make Dwell better and better for the user. They are lifelong learners *(and friends)*, and they continue to make those around them better.

Another amazing group I've recently been a part of is known as

GoBundance. It's a tribe of wise and motivated men that are all sharing invaluable knowledge and pushing one another to be better, not only for ourselves but for our wives, families, and community. I'm amazed that I can ask questions to the tribe and get answers quickly and candidly. A big reason for this book coming to fruition was the motivation from a bi-weekly video chat with other authors. During the call, everyone would talk about what was working for them, next steps, and how we can help get each other to the word count destination we desired. I can't stress enough how important it is to have people around you that motivate and believe in you. With the right people in your corner your impossibles become possible.

This collection of incredible people might not know it, but I've been watching them for thirty-six years now. From the warm-hearted church I grew up in, to the generous teachers and coaches that molded me, these amazing people have made me who I am. There's gratitude and confidence pouring out through my fingers as I write this. Without these great mentors to learn from, my life would not be anywhere near where it is today. I am better because of those who have selflessly poured into me.

I know there are many individuals that I have not specifically mentioned in this book but those people are not forgotten. I feel as though I could write an entire book of thank you notes from me to everyone who has guided me along my journey. From everything within me I graciously say thank you!

The lessons your mentors have passed on to you are worth more than you can imagine. Be grateful for these all too often invisible mentors you've have in your life. Learn to see and value these people for all they are. These valuable guides in your life add up to something visible: a life well-lived.

TOOTHPASTE FOR POMADE

Toothpaste for pomade? Sounds pretty ridiculous, right? Why would anyone ever try to use pomade to brush his teeth? No one *(that I know of)* does this, and it's because you were taught what pomade is to be used for, either by someone close to you or by reading the label. The instructions on the jar tell you exactly how to use it. In fact, without directions on products, most people would have to experiment with how they are to be used. That's a pretty scary thought, right? Think about it, people would probably experiment by using laundry soap for baking, tic tacs as suppositories, or peanut butter for makeup. There would be a plethora of overly weird internet videos and most likely rampant lawsuits. Lucky for the rest of us, people have already figured these things out. Those who designed these items or learned how to use them teach the rest of us how to use these products. When one person learns how to use something, they pass along that knowledge to the next. It doesn't mean we can't question use or what is being taught, but this relayed information gives us a foundation to work from.

When you buy something new, if you don't know how to use it, you read the directions or find a video explaining how to use it. Or you can always ask someone with experience. You then observe, learn how to do it, and then it's easier the next time around. Why not take this method and apply it to everything? Learn to admit when you don't know something, and then just be quiet and listen. Desire to be taught. Ask someone to teach you how to do something you know nothing about. This not only allows you to advance in life, but once again, it gives value to the person teaching you. It's a win-win.

So, next time you see a jar of pomade, think about how lucky you are that you don't have to figure out that it's not toothpaste. That nasty taste in your mouth would surely linger for far too long. Someone already figured this out for you in advance, to help you have a better life. Be humble enough to recognize this truth, and then open your mind to learn from other people.

Chapter Six

FAILING FORWARD

"Failure should be our teacher, not our undertaker. Failure is delay, not defeat. It is a temporary detour, not a dead end."

- Denis Waitley

Have you ever talked to someone about or researched the topic of debt? People say that debt, when used correctly, can lead to the creation of wealth. But if used incorrectly, debt can lead to financial ruin. Same tool, two very different results. I've seen both sides of this coin.

I've witnessed first-hand how to use debt incorrectly. Terrible financial advice was given and too many liabilities were purchased. I witnessed numerous people stack bad debt by way of a second home, meaningless equipment, toys, and anything else you can imagine. Everything seems fine until the main source of income is lost. Then the debt spiral begins. With no steady income from a paycheck and no cash flow coming in from the liabilities, it's a quick trip to the bottom. The leveraged houses, toys, and miscellaneous all come due. Everything that was owned, is now impossible to keep. The bad debt is crippling.

I have also witnessed how to use debt correctly for the creation of wealth. It can be invested into a business or real estate portfolio and produce meaningful income. For example, in real estate debt can be taken out on a rental property through a conventional bank loan. Over the course of twenty-five years, that debt can be paid off by the multiple tenants of the property. During the period in which the debt is being paid off, the property has a chance to appreciate in value, and you can take depreciation on the asset against your taxes. The asset produces passive income, and your debt will eventually paid off. Without debt, you probably could not have afforded the asset to begin with. So in this case, debt is a good thing. Same tool, very different result in the end.

The same concept can be applied to failure. If failure is leveraged in such a way that you see and understand its value and make up your mind to decide to grow from failures, your future can be significantly different and the possibilities will be endless. On the contrary, if you allow failures to stack up and you feel that you're a failure because of them, you can cause great harm to yourself and those around you. Failures can be a catalyst for growth, or failures can lead to self-pity, stress, and destruction. It's all about your perspective. Same tool, two very different results.

Liz Wiseman used this concept to write the book *Multipliers* in 2010. She concluded that leaders can be placed into two categories: multipliers or diminishers. Multipliers add to the people around them and make them smarter and more capable. Diminishers, however, take away from their people and cripple their functioning and growth. There is a massive difference in the two directions, but a multiplication effect either way. A leader or boss can get more productivity and passion out of fewer people, or they can get less out of more. Multipliers build the confidence of the people they serve and give them the confidence to work through problems without the fear of failure. The multiplier, according to Wiseman, is an investor in people. In her book, Liz states, "It isn't how much you know that matters. What matters is how much access you have to what other people know."[11] That's one of my favorite quotes from her book. She's saying that having access to other people's experiences and wisdom, without the fear of condemnation, is vital to company growth. Just as the access to information is vital to a company's culture, it's key to your personal growth as well. Knowing is very important, and you want to know and grow, but having access to other people's base of knowledge is an asset. If you can get full access to learn from other people's failures, you will quickly multiply your growth in a positive direction. Remember, you don't have to experience failure in order to learn from it.

FAILURE ISN'T AN OPTION, IT'S A REQUIREMENT

When people actively try to avoid failure, they severely stunt their growth and potential. Without failure, people can get comfortable–much too comfortable. When people are comfortable, they have very little reason to improve. They prevent themselves from making any sort of progress. There are times when this is caused by inaction due to striving for perfection. Expecting perfection always causes mental and emotional instability. Don't expect perfection but relish in temporary failure. The process of failing is not a failure unless you stay where you are. To grow, you must learn from your own mistakes and the mistakes of others. You can still learn from success, but success tends to make us lazy. It takes a special person to learn from success and not let it go to her head. Even if you can learn from success, there will always be plenty of room for more growth by learning from failures.

Have you ever thought about when babies learn to walk? They are very unstable, but also very close to the ground. They try to walk and often fall, over and over again. Since they are so close to the ground, the fall doesn't hurt them compared to if they were falling from a higher height. Babies don't try to learn how to walk on the top of a two-story building with no railing. If the first chance they had to fail was to fall from a great height, learning to walk wouldn't work. The risk would be too great. Toddlers need small failures that they can learn from, day in and day out. Eventually, if all goes well, they will succeed. Little failures and the lessons they come with will lead to success. Little failures often deflate bigger failures. Learn to fail in small ways, and then consciously learn from those actions to avoid failing in bigger situations.

If failure is a requirement, you need a good way to manage the stress that comes with failure. A great way to change your mindset and deal with the stress of failure is to learn to laugh at yourself. A lot of people take themselves way too seriously all the time. They don't have the ability to laugh at a mistake or have the confidence to lean into a mistake in front of others and learn from it. Epictetus once said, "He who laughs at himself never runs out of things to laugh at."[12] Learning to laugh at and with yourself will produce a mindset where you don't care if you fail, as long as you're learning. You can fail, learn, and laugh along the way. As you're laughing, you understand that you're on your way to becoming a better person. Learning to laugh at yourself and your own failures is a difficult skill to learn and master. However, if you can master how to laugh and learn when you fail, you will be better for it.

CONFIDENCE IN FAILURE

Mitch McHenry is the current high school boys basketball coach at Kickapoo High School here in my hometown of Springfield, Missouri. Mitch was, and still is, a phenomenal athlete. I've had the opportunity to play with him in a handful of flag football tournaments and witnessed how he carries himself and those that play with him. Mitch has a confidence about him that overflows to others. When someone makes a mistake, he doesn't throw his hands up in disgust but patiently waits for the right moment to teach. This translated very well to his high school coaching career. In 2021, Kickapoo High School won the Missouri Class 6 state basketball championship. In a recent conversation with Mitch, I congratulated him on the championship, and he promptly deflected any sort of praise. He said it was due to the fact that the team had high-caliber players, and said that he only played a small role.

I quickly spoke about his role and said that I knew he had a lot more to do with it than he led on. I have been a part of and seen teams with great players lose more often than win. I have seen great players shrivel under the weight of a terrible leader and coach. Mitch is a special person and coach who understands how to have confidence in failure, in both himself and in his athletes. He leads in a way that elevates teammates. He coaches in a way that produces confidence in his players, through failures and success. That confidence is established in practice, and it shows up on game day. The players under his guidance are better for it individually and as a team. Mitch is a professional failure that helps those around him greatly improve. And he is all the more successful because of it. He will go as far as he wants to go in the coaching profession because he will never stop learning, improving, and making those around him the best they can be.

If you are learning from your failure, you must have certain confidence along with it. You have to know that in the midst of your failure, that perceived failure still has a purpose. You still have a purpose, and the failure you're experiencing doesn't define you. You can't get lost in the dark moments and forget about where you're going. The goal is personal growth, not perfection every single time. When you have a mindset to learn, you can simply shift your emotional thinking from, "I'm ashamed and embarrassed because I failed," to "What can I learn from this experience?" It doesn't matter what other people think. It doesn't matter if they don't understand and think you're a loser for not getting it right. That's the level of confidence you seek to possess. If people think you're unintelligent for asking a question, it doesn't matter. If people are disappointed in you because you failed at a specific moment, it doesn't matter. Learn from that moment and become better for the next moment that arises. If people expect you to be perfect and never make mistakes, that doesn't matter either. No one will ever be perfect. Perfection in life is unattainable. What matters is how you see yourself, where you're going, and who's helping you improve.

You also need to be cognizant of who you're going to help improve along the way as well. You can't be a know-it-all, but you can be a great resource when people are ready to learn. As you improve, you'll improve the lives of those around you as well. The more you improve, the more people will take notice and want to be around you. If you can show confidence through failures and confidence in yourself, it will transfer to others. People will take notice of how you live and face failure. The more confidence you possess, the more people you can help. When combined with humility, your confidence will become an encouragement to others. You can improve the lives of other people by simply having confidence in yourself.

Seeing the abundance of potential in failure will help you to build your confidence. When a person flat out fails at something, most witnesses see that moment and simply try to associate it with the person involved in the failure. All those involved need to remember that the failure was temporary. If you can rise above that mediocrity and realize the God-given potential in each moment, you will take your confidence to new heights. You'll be able to see the potential in the mess and find beauty in failure.

It's not a fun feeling when everyone around you doesn't understand or see what you see. The situation can seem lonely at first, but there's no need to be defensive or calloused. I joke about this when I like a certain food or drink that other people don't like. For instance, I really like pickled okra. Most people say, "That's gross! I can't believe you eat that." Instead of thinking that I'm weird, I can simply reply, "Good! More for me! It's a blessing that you don't like this because that means I don't have to worry about you stealing my pickled okra!"

Oftentimes seeing things from a different perspective is a great tool to have in your arsenal. Even if most people don't see it, it really doesn't matter. You need to learn to be able to see whatever problem or situation you're facing from a different perspective. Learn to value and see the massive opportunities in failure. Failure can be a blessing. Let that blessing build your confidence. You have every ability to learn and grow from the mistakes you witness and make along the way. Trust me, you will be better for it in the long run.

LEVERAGING FAILURES

Once I consciously began to learn and accumulate the abundance of knowledge from those around me, the next question was: is it possible to leverage failure? When thinking about how to properly leverage failure, you need to think about the future and not the present. It's important to be present, but with expectant eyes on the harvest of the future. I use a lot of farmer analogies because I grew up around farmers. The mindset of the farmer is simple: do today what will produce a harvest in the future. Put in the work now so you can reap the rewards later. If a farmer plants a seed and then impatiently comes back the next day to see that nothing has happened, what is his response? Does he have the wisdom to know that growth takes time, or is he discouraged because there's no evidence of growth yet?

The farmer understands that growth is taking place underground, something not yet seen, and that the harvest will be coming at a later time. The farmer is present but has his eyes toward the future. He nurtures the seedling when nothing is visible and when the seed sprouts, he takes care of the delicate plant even when it's not yet bearing fruit.

When the harvest does come, the farmer gets feedback on what kind of job he has done along the way. There are always obstacles when farming, but the farmer learns to overcome them. The farmer learns from what works and what doesn't. He enjoys the harvest because he understands what it took for the harvest to happen. His wise perspective allows him to not get caught up in the present and to anticipate the future harvest.

Failure can be a beautiful thing, just as planting a small seed can produce a beautiful crop. It's about nurturing what you can't yet see and preparing for the harvest. When you experience failure, do you focus on the present embarrassment or self-pity, or are you fully present with eyes towards the future? Do you often get impatient when expected results don't happen right away? I still struggle with patience and embarrassment, but I continue to work on it. Answering these questions for yourself and embedding the farmer's mentality into your mind will produce a beautiful harvest. With the correct perspective, you can build your confidence through failure and focus on what lessons learned will lead to down the road.

Think of your coming harvest as sprouting doors of opportunity. You planted small seedlings, and they're growing into many opportunities. When they are full grown, you'll be able to walk through that door to the other side of a new opportunity. You don't really know what door will open for you, but having options is rarely a bad thing.

FREEDOM TO LOOK STUPID
ON THE PATH TO SUCCESS

What if you were able to ask any question to anyone without the fear of looking dumb? How many questions would you ask with a simple goal to learn? How fast could you learn? What if I told you that specific skill is available to you now? Learn to ask the right questions, without the crippling fear of looking unintelligent, and the world will open up to you. There is so much information available to us all if we simply learn to ask without fear.

When children learn, they soak up anything and everything. They ask numerous questions to the point of being annoying. It's not because they're trying to upset you or trying to annoy you, but they are genuinely curious and want to learn. They need to learn. They don't care that the questions they're asking may make them look unintelligent because their focused mission is to grow, both physically and mentally. When children get scolded for asking questions or made fun of because they don't know an answer, it can greatly stunt their learning and growth. The children that continue to ask questions are the ones that find success in their pursuit of knowledge or a skill. The key is to be more like a child and continue asking questions, no matter how unintelligent you may seem to an observer.

When children become adults, more often than not, they lose this sense of curiosity and questioning. Somewhere along the way to adulthood, the fear of looking unintelligent forms into a debilitating monster. It could start in elementary school, where the teacher asks a simple question. A student answers incorrectly and laughter from his classmates ensues.

It could start at home when a young child asks a parent for help and instead of lovingly helping, the parent talks down to the child and sarcastically asks how she doesn't know that already. Instead of earnestly teaching, that parent plants a seed of fear: the fear of looking dumb. Children remember these moments and the pain or embarrassment that accompanies them. As children grow into adults, the moments compound on one another. They may now be fearful of looking dumb in front of a boss, client, or family member. They may hesitate to ask a relevant question because they don't want to offend someone. Whatever the reason is, they simply stop asking. This is the hindrance of most people and a big reason why they slow their pace of learning. They care more about keeping their superficial intelligence intact rather than actually being intelligent and learning new things. It's a short-term gain for a long-term problem.

Think through this: would you rather be the most unintelligent person in the world and known as the wisest, or be the wisest person in the world and known as the most unintelligent? Answer that for yourself and keep that in your mind going forward. When you ask a question that makes you seem unintelligent, know that you're on your way to being wise, even if you have the disguise of unintelligence.

Ward Cunningham came up with an interesting concept that was soon named after him. If you've never heard of Cunningham's Law, it's perfectly fine. I hadn't heard of the law either until doing research for this book. In summary, Cunningham's Law states, *"The best way to get the right answer on the internet is not to ask a question; it's to post the wrong answer.*[13] When you post something incorrect online, you get a flood of people rushing in to prove how smart they are. It can be overwhelming. They're out to prove how dumb you are compared to how intelligent they are. It's a sad sign of the state of most people's grace and understanding. Instead of helping and encouraging, they diminish your intellect in order to boost their own. If you have thick skin, feel free to test this law online. You'll soon learn who is encouraging and who is seeking to prop themselves up by pushing you down. Don't take it personally, most people don't even realize what they're doing.

Going a bit further on Cunningham's Law, what if you take this concept outside the realm of the internet and into real life? Make an incorrect statement and allow someone to correct you. Don't be defensive, just be quiet and listen. Avoid saying, "I knew that!" at the end and just take an intellectual scolding. It's good for you and even though your ego may be hurting, you'll build your confidence muscle through this process. Once you've had some practice with that, turn your statements into questions. Instead of making statements that you know are incorrect, start asking questions that seem to reference the "wrong" answer.

An example could be, "I've heard there is a fourth element to water." If you decide to give this a go, prepare for weird looks and funny rabbit holes. Enjoy the odd moments and build your confidence in asking questions. If nothing else, it's an amazing conversation starter. As you'll soon learn, it's very possible to be wise without looking the part. You can have a quiet wisdom without loudly declaring to the world that you know more than they do.

Looking back, I remember several times in my life when I asked simple questions because I didn't understand the problem or situation. Instead of feeling ashamed that I didn't know, I felt an excitement that I had a chance to learn. Even if I was intellectually lost, it didn't matter. I wanted to understand the concept. I just asked the dumb question. Funny enough, sometimes the people explaining the matter couldn't explain it to me either! They didn't fully understand it themselves, yet expected me to understand. Don't grow weary in asking seemingly dumb questions. I missed plenty of opportunities growing up that could have accelerated my learning and I still do. Don't worry about missing opportunities, just focus on correcting it going forward. Practice asking questions and be aware of how much your understanding of that particular subject deepens.

For another exercise, try this: the next time you're in a conversation with someone, try to ask a basic question that you already know the answer to. Ask questions and let your conversation partner answer you. Allow them to teach you in a subject you're very familiar with. To take it a step further, think of Cunningham's Law, and make a statement that you know is likely incorrect. See what happens and where the discussion leads. Did your conversation partner answer you in a kind, loving way, or did they degrade you by saying, "You don't know that already?!" or by rolling his eyes? Take note of these interactions with other people and yourself. You want to be around people who care enough to pour encouragement and life into you and not the people that make you feel stupid. You also need to learn to be someone who lovingly teaches and doesn't make others feel stupid. Remember, the more you give away, the more that comes back to you. Teach people and they will in turn teach you.

Chapter Seven

MAKING NEW CONNECTIONS

"We are what we repeatedly do.
Excellence, therefore, is not an act,
but a habit."

- Aristotle

A crucial part of learning from others is making new connections in your brain–new connections that you were not previously aware of. You might have had the information in your mind but never, as the old idiom goes, "put two and two together" in your head. Connecting knowledge from one area to another is the foundation of wisdom. The more information you possess and evaluate, the better your problem-solving will be. Your brain is powerful enough to store unlimited amounts of information, so use it and learn to stretch its abilities. You don't have to learn everything at once, but as you go, be aware of the relationship between new and old information.

What is the brain's process of making new connections? Upon learning new connections, your brain will literally rewire itself as you learn and create new pathways. In creating new pathways, you grow in capacity and wisdom. This opens the door to even more connections down the road and is a great multiplier of your success. With new connections come new opportunities, new conversations, and new people in your life. These new opportunities and conversations can lead to even more knowledge and opportunities. As you make new connections, you also become a better resource for those around you. People will soon request your presence, and you will play a vital role in the conversation. When you share these connections, people will often share new information back with you. The more connections you make, the bigger the foundation you're able to construct. The quality of people you attract and learn from will also improve.

When people have that "Aha!" moment, they are making a new connection. They have successfully linked two new ideas in their brains. It's just like finding that piece to a puzzle that fits perfectly. It's always been there, available to you, but now you see it and put it to use. Learn to train your brain to think about connecting ideas. Making new connections doesn't have to be a solo adventure. Understand that if you don't have the answer, someone else may have what you're searching for. When you make new connections with another person or a team, everyone learns together. New connections and growth are experienced by everyone involved, not just a single person. Seek to make new connections with other people, and put those ideas to work.

Let's look at this connection process in more detail. Athletes, musicians, and dancers all train. They all learn, and they all form habits based on repetitive behaviors. This repetition forms new connections in your brain. The new connections help strengthen old pathways and improve your ability to do a simple task or perform at a high level. Habits allow baseball players to dive and catch a ball in midair, or a musician to play the guitar and sing at the same time. In most cases, the more the habit has been practiced and put on autopilot, the better the performer's outcome.

According to an article by *Science News for Students*, doing something repeatedly doesn't just make things easier, it actually changes the wiring in your brain.[14] This rewiring is strong in children, but most people think that if you're above a certain age, your ability to learn decreases significantly. That's simply not true. People just become set in their ways and don't want to learn anymore, using, "I can't," as an excuse. Scientists once thought that our brains stopped this rewiring process once we hit a certain age, but they have since debunked that.[15]

It's no longer the easy excuse not to learn anything new. No matter how old you are, you're never too old to learn! It also means that the responsibility is fully on you. No more excuses. Learning can be messy and slow at first on your own, but watching and learning from someone who has already made the mistakes, or learned from someone else, can help speed up the process. You're never too young or old to learn, and the brain is constantly making new connections. New connections form whether you're aware of them or not. If your brain is constantly making new connections, you might as well make connections that will improve your life and the lives of those around you. The brain is a gift: a high-functioning, never-to-be-duplicated precious gift. Take full advantage of what you've been gifted and start making new, conscious connections.

This extraordinary habit-forming ability obviously works apart from athletics as well. Learning a new piece of information from history or economics allows the many connections in your brain to develop. These new pieces of information become ingrained in our thinking and ability to recall the information in future conversations. You can connect new and old concepts and see the world in a new light, sometimes with perceived ease–ease of thinking that you didn't have access to before. You're literally building a database in your head. Once the information is there, you can begin to search through your inventory, and process ideas and situations with greater accuracy and speed. After all, wisdom is simplicity! Wisdom is just simplifying complex subjects in your mind. The new connections you make when learning become like second nature and your thoughts become more effortless.

See these connections as bridges in your mind. If you need to cross a gap without a bridge, it's going to be tough. You either have to jump an extraordinary distance or figure out another way to go around. If you already have a bridge built, it's a simple walk across, almost effortless. Learn to build bridges in your mind and allow yourself to simply walk across them.

Understanding how making new connections affects your brain, it's now vitally important what goes into your mind. If you are filling up your mind with lies, rather than facts, the connections you make might be strong, but they will be false. Let's go ahead and call these false connections. They're very unstable. You may think you understand a certain subject, but if you build your understanding on half-lies and half-truth, what do you have? You have a working knowledge of something that is built on sand. When someone challenges your connection, you either have to concede that you are wrong and learn from it, or dig in and prove that you are right. The greater the number of lies you learn and take as truth, the greater your confusion will be later on down the road. You must learn the correct information (and not the half-lies) from the beginning. Be hyper aware of what goes into your mind when learning. Mistakes will happen but you need to have the mental fortitude to correct them when they do.

Like I mentioned earlier, making new connections is a multiplier. When you learn something new, your brain has the incredible ability to reach into storage and pull from another memory or thought, and then connect that to the new thing you learned. The brain is made up of billions of neurons that talk to each other using chemical messengers. The neurons fire off messages, and after time, these messages become more efficient.[16] This explains how when athletes repeatedly practice certain actions, those actions eventually become second nature. They can perform these feats with little or no thought, as if on autopilot. This allows someone to build on previously learned behaviors and stack complex actions together. For example, a quarterback in football can run laterally, and visually read the defense. He then mentally works through what the best chance of a completion would be to a receiver *(that is also running)*, and finally, with a little help from the receiver, complete the pass. That is an extraordinary athletic accomplishment. These actions are stacked behaviors. The ability is gained gradually through practice, not all at once. The brain stores away new abilities, becomes more efficient and shifts its focus to new tasks. Without this stacking ability, we would not be the high-functioning society and individuals we are today.

Your brain doesn't stop learning while you're inactive either. It's a supercomputer when you're asleep as well. When we sleep, our brain stores and organizes the things we have learned that day. Do you understand how amazing this is?! Your brain continues to process and become more efficient even when you're not trying. This subconscious sorting of information has led to numerous scientific breakthroughs and also helped you remember that person's name at the gathering. Nikola Tesla, the famous electrical scientist and inventor, was said to have built up his inventions in his mind expecting his subconscious to later reveal how to build it to his conscious mind. He trusted his subconscious so much that he didn't worry about the details of his inventions and simply moved forward, having faith that his mind would sort it out.[17] And it wasn't just Tesla, Einstein and Edison are known to have worked out problems in their sleep as well![18] Pretty amazing. What's even more amazing is that you have that same ability. Yes, you! Your mind was built just like Tesla's. He may have perfected how to use it at a high level, but it's still the same brain. It's ready to be put to work for you as well.

The brain has so much ability and power, the question in my mind becomes: why not test its capabilities? How much can we consciously and unconsciously learn in our lifetimes? And what is the downside of learning all these lessons and habits? How much ability does our brain possess that we can't comprehend? The world's fastest supercomputer is still no match for the human brain's design. The more you learn, the more doors that will be opened. Not just for you, but for others as well. Why not share those discoveries *(and multiply them exponentially)* with other people that see the world in a slightly different way? When you share your connections with other people, it opens up new ways of thinking and possibilities. Connections are not meant to be kept to yourself. The more you share, the greater the chance you have of growing.

THE VELOCITY OF KNOWLEDGE AND POWER

•

The velocity of money is how quickly money changes hands in an economy. The faster the transfer of money, the healthier an economy is said to be. The lower the velocity of money, the more likely it is that a contraction or recession will occur. Economies that display a higher velocity of money tend to be more developed. And when economies hold on to money, the economy tends to grow smaller and weaker. When money moves quickly, the economy is healthy and growing. It's not necessarily about how much money is available, just how fast it is circulating.

I believe that knowledge and power work the same way, even though most people might not realize it. Let's first look at knowledge. When you freely give knowledge to others and help them get what they want, you tend to get things in return. Zig Ziglar famously said, *"You will get all you want in life, if you help enough other people get what they want."*[19] Give and then receive. That's not to say you can't charge for your knowledge or expertise, because you can in some cases and you should. But when you start providing great knowledge and insight to other people and they, in turn, pass it along, it can not only help you, but it can help an entire community.[20] Civilizations of the past and present were built by passing along knowledge from one generation to the next. Knowledge is power, and I believe both are meant to be shared, not selfishly held onto.

What about the velocity of power? I've witnessed individuals and organizations hold on tightly to power, only concerned with themselves and not the well being of those around them. It seems like a constant struggle for power and those companies or individuals seem to have very weak relationships. Those relationships are easily broken by higher salaries, more freedom, or revolt. The success they have seems to only last for a short period of time. All the secrecy and back-stabbing usually catches up with them.

Ironically, if those in charge simply empowered those around them, the lives of the people holding on to power would be dramatically improved as well. When an individual finally makes it to a place of power, it's not wrong, but that person does have a responsibility: a massive responsibility to empower others. They will become a multiplier or a diminisher. And when you empower others through knowledge, you make the lives of all around you better, including your own.

My dad told me growing up that when he hired people, he would always try and hire someone better than him. He wasn't afraid of not looking smart or someone passing him in the ranks, but he wanted a great team around him. When you have a great team, it takes pressure off of you. You don't have to carry the load all by yourself. Looking back, it was a lesson in leadership and humility. He did this to help the company he owned work for better and make his job a little easier. Too many people are scared to empower others because they feel it will make them unimportant or expendable. This is nothing more than a lie. When you empower others, you become a resource that other people think of when they need help. The more value you provide to others, the better your life will be.

Is it possible to share too much information? Has someone ever been robbed of an idea or let go because of freely passing along knowledge or power? Yes, no doubt, but that reveals something even more valuable to me. If you give away information and power to other people and they stab you in the back, you learn quickly who you can trust.

Having people around you that you know you can trust is worth more than gold. It's the foundation that castles are built upon. If it's hard to trust people on the small things, it will be impossible to trust those same people with big things. Weed them out. Figure out who you can trust as soon as you can, the earlier the better. Losing an idea in the short term, for the long term gain of knowing who you can trust, is well worth the tradeoff.

I believe the Bible also teaches us about this velocity. One parable is of the evil servant who buried his money (Matthew 25:18). Three servants are given the same amount of money by their master, who goes away for a time. Two servants invest what they have been given and bring back more money than what they started with. Those two servants were applauded and praised by their master. The third servant hid the money for fear of losing it and facing harsh consequences. This bad servant was scolded by his master and called evil. The money that was given to him was taken away and that same money was given to the other servants who stewarded the money well to begin with.

This parable could be referring to souls, money, or possibly something else. Any way you see it, the story should have an "aha" moment for you. What good is money if you store it up and never share it with others? What good is wisdom if you only collect and possess it for your own gain? If you only use money, power, or knowledge for yourself, just to build your own kingdom, what value does that bring in the end? When you put these things in motion, either by a solid investment or by giving it away, it can produce value. Value that would have not existed if you simply hid your resources away for fear of losing them. That value can be magnified by an investment in others or by simply sharing the resources you've been blessed with.

The point is, don't let the fear of losing money or power push you into hiding it under your mattress or keeping it away from others. Your very own resources of money and wisdom can and should be invested. It can't be said enough, money is simply a tool. Beyond just money, wisdom and power are tools. These tools can be used for evil, but they can also be used for good. Learn to use your tools of money, wisdom, and power in a way that benefits those around you. You're planting seeds with sound investments and other people, and what you give will come back to you. This is the velocity of knowledge and power. You get and you give. Grow this mindset. If you can harness its ability, you will add immense value to your life and the lives of those close to you.

THE POWER OF A GOOD QUESTION

Simply asking a good question in order to start a conversation or in the middle of one is often overlooked. A simple question is often engaging and powerful, and there is unlimited potential when you ask a great question. The right question can turn around a conversation immediately and can lead to candid responses from private people. When you ask good questions in a conversation, you pique the curiosity and the attentiveness of your conversation mate. When you ask bad questions, you get short-winded answers that bring little, if any, to the conversation. The way you ask questions, and the responses you receive, hinges on other factors as well. Body language and eye contact are two of the most important. You can't just ask a question while looking at your phone–that often isn't received very well. Good eye contact amplifies the power of a good question. When you are successfully engaged in a conversation, a good question can bring the discussion to another level.

One of the keys to asking a good question is curiosity. When you're curious about another individual or subject, you pay attention to more details and have a desire to learn attentively. You also ask better questions. Your brain activates and ideas flow naturally. Better questions bring better answers, which leads to more curiosity and ultimately more ideas–ideas for deeper discussions or genuine interest in another person. This curiosity allows you to stay tuned into the conversation without having to pick up your phone and check the latest update from your seventeen social media accounts. When you're curious and interested in your conversation partners' hobbies and interests, they will often open up and talk more. People like talking about what they know and love talking about what they're interested in. The key for you is to genuinely find interest in their passions during the conversation. It doesn't mean you have to go out and take up another hobby, but during the chat, you can be fully engaged and in awe of what you don't know. It is possible to be genuinely interested in a subject you know nothing about or don't plan on learning any more about after the conversation. When you're curious, you're engaged, and when you're engaged, you ask great questions.

Meaningful questions are a portal into someone's life. Are there immoral people that will lie to your face or dodge a good question? Absolutely. But don't let that stop you. If you're asking the right question and you get a sense that someone isn't being truthful, either ask more questions until he breaks or get away from him! It's fairly easy to walk away from a stranger that isn't being truthful, but when someone close to you is lying, it gets complicated and can be very hurtful. You have to learn to rise above it. Asking good questions can break down barriers and asking the right questions can restore relationships.

Asking thoughtful questions also allows you to steer the conversation in the direction you want. If you're in a conversation and you ~~~~~~ it's headed, ask a pivot question and gently guide the ~~~~~ her topic. This is taught in the tactics of negotiat~~~~~~ one of the key ways negotiators gather information and form strategies. A negotiator can also implement and share her point of view through questioning, rather than lecturing the counterpart on what they should do. The questions are disarming and allow the counterpart to respond and not be overly defensive. It's one of the most important and effective ways to talk through a heated situation. If a trained negotiator values questions this highly, you should be paying close attention.

The finishing work in asking questions is listening. If you ask a question and then turn your eyes to the table next to you, your non-verbal cues tell your counterpart that you're not interested. Trust me, I've done this before, and it's a conversation killer if someone is paying attention to what's going on. A friend and I were having a casual discussion and for some reason, my mind started to wander. I asked a question and when my friend started to answer, my mind drifted. He spoke for about thirty seconds and then realized what was happening. To his credit, he didn't attack me, he just simply asked me a question in reference to what he was talking about. I had no answer. I felt ashamed and awful for wasting his time. We ended the conversation shortly thereafter and went on with our days. Lucky for me he's an amazing man, and we're still good friends to this day. He showed me grace and it was a very beneficial lesson for me. If you're in a conversation, be present and curious, as this gives needed value to your friend or counterpart in the discussion. I can't stress it enough, *pay attention when someone is speaking*, so you can thoughtfully and coherently respo and ask the right questions when the time comes.

Chapter Eight

PERFECTION IS POISON

"Perfectionism rarely begets perfection, or satisfaction - only disappointment."

- Ryan Holiday

Do you have friends that just can't seem to get out of their own way? They have all the talent and skills needed, but they can't take that first step towards a better life. They allow fear, excuses, and the pursuit of perfection to stop them from doing anything. When you allow perfection to be your idol and cripple yourself by not starting, it hinders you in a mighty way. Not only do you miss out on the potential of doing great things, but you miss out on the journey of learning. You don't have to be perfect to succeed; no one ever is! It's the people that understand that perfection is the enemy that proceed to learn, grow, and do great things.

What I've learned is that action tends to compound opportunities. When you're not worried about being perfect, you can be confident in taking action. That means you simply start, even though you might not have all the details figured out. When you take action, you often learn from more experiences and action leads to great teachers, if you'll pay attention. As it's been said for generations, it's always easier to turn a moving car than one that's sitting still. Those many experiences lead to opportunities–*opportunities that were previously out of reach*. Opportunities that you would not have had if you had not started moving forward. The next time you wonder why you don't have the same opportunities as others, look introspectively and ask yourself if you're taking action or waiting until the perfect situation (or you) presents itself?

In his book *Limitless*, Jim Kwik writes about how each one of us has the potential to learn. Not just learn, but learn in a big way. Jim had a traumatic brain injury as a kid and was even labeled "the kid with a broken brain" by a teacher. He couldn't focus in school and couldn't read properly early on. He now coaches athletes, celebrities, and people all around the world on how to get more out of reading, memorization, and life in general. If you haven't read his book or seen his story, you should put this book down right now and go read it.[21] Jim states in his book that, "Perfectionism reduces creativity and innovation." I would go a step further and say that perfectionism kills creativity and innovation. When someone is laser focused on perfection, it often leads to paralysis by analysis. People don't take action because they're afraid to make a mistake. It is nearly impossible to learn in this manner and even if you do, the rate at which someone learns is dramatically reduced. Chasing perfection is not a good place to be if your goal is to learn. You need to focus on striving to do a great job but not be perfect. Perfect gets in the way of learning.

Jim also states that there is no such thing as a good or bad brain, only a trained and untrained brain. Think of how many people you know demean themselves and say they're terrible at remembering things or that they just have a bad memory. That negative thinking seeps into your brain and you actually listen to yourself! If you want to become better at memorizing names or remembering dates, train your brain to do those tasks. You do have a capability to carry out these tasks, you just might be underestimating your ability.

An article by Mel Schwartz entitled "The Problem with Perfection" also touches on the subject of perfection. It begins by stating that "the desire to be perfect burdens many people and ironically dooms them to unhappiness."[22] If we are all chasing happiness, then why are we messing around with trying to be perfect? A perfect score of 100% on a test might be one thing, but trying to be perfect in life is completely different. That means you have no flaws and never make mistakes. Not only is that not attainable, but imagine the amount of pressure that being perfect or striving to be perfect brings. The article goes on to say that we need to "embrace the imperfection of being human." That doesn't mean that we go out and mess up in every area of our lives just to learn. One does not need to go out and cheat on his spouse in order to learn a lesson from it. That's why we have mentors, morals, and laws to help guide us. There are many things in life that we don't have to experience ourselves in order to learn a valuable lesson.

Just remember, perfection can be an enemy and a gigantic road-block to learning. When you try to be perfect, it causes you to take less action, experience more stress, make less mistakes, and ultimately learn a lot less in the process. I can't remember who told me this along the way, or where I read it, but the phrase "done is better than perfect" always stuck with me. Complete a task, learn from the process, and do it better the next time around.

DON'T BE SMART, BE A LEARNER

My wife and I do not have the honor of having kids at this point in our lives. Even though we don't have children yet, I've had the opportunity to watch and learn from many different parents over the past fifteen years. *Remember, just because you're not in someone else's specific situation, doesn't mean you can't learn from that person.* One concerning thing I've noticed is how mentally detrimental it is for parents to brag about their kids being smart. It puts so much pressure on the kids to have to know everything because if they don't know, they feel unintelligent. This can often lead to being intimidated of trying new things or simply a decreased desire in new experiences. If you've learned nothing else please remember that if you don't try and fail, or learn from the failure of others, personal growth and consistent progress will elude you. I see so many kids with so much potential, but their parents have instilled a fear of failure into them. With this instilled mindset at such a young age, it will be hard for them to break out of this way of thinking unless they rebel against their upbringing. Kids need to have a healthy relationship with failure and a mindset of effort, even when there's a high probability they won't succeed in the beginning. It's a simple formula: the more kids try without fear of failure, the more they learn and the less kids try, the less likely they are to learn.

Parents obviously don't mean any harm by calling their children smart, but they don't really think about what it can do to their child's progress and future. If calling a kid smart isn't a good way to brag on a child, what can be done differently? Instead of parents and other adults telling children that they are smart for figuring out a problem or puzzle, why not encourage them by telling them you're proud of their resilience in figuring out the problem? Encourage the incredible effort and not the result. The difference between calling children smart and encouraging their effort and perseverance is massive. From my research, the psychology behind the action can affect children for years, and unfortunately, build habits that are nearly impossible to break when they're older.

There are numerous articles written on how calling kids smart affects their mental well being. You may have already come across them without giving them any second thought. One article written by James Hambiln for The Atlantic states, "People labeled smart at a young age don't do well with being wrong." What have we learned about being afraid of failure? If people learn to fear failure, they stunt their growth. If kids can't handle being wrong, then they probably won't try new things and stretch their mental and physical capabilities. They will still grow and learn, but not at the same pace as other kids who aren't afraid to fail. Those same kids also tend to push that fear of failure onto other children. Later in the article, it goes on to say, *"When we give kids the message that mistakes are good, that successful people make mistakes, it can change their entire trajectory."*[23] When we inform kids that messing up is a part of the process and is to be expected, what kind of impact can that bring? When children know they don't have to be perfect in order to be viewed as intelligent, the sky's the limit! It changes their mindset going into a problem and allows them to take risks in learning. Just because kids don't get the right answer, doesn't mean they aren't smart, it just means they're trying new things and haven't learned that new skill or bit of information.

Based on another study by a group of psychologists, it can get worse than just a fear of failure. In an article by Romper entitled "How Calling Your Kid Smart Could Actually Hurt Them Later In Life," a study reveals when children are praised for being smart or are told that they have a reputation for it, they feel pressure to perform well to live up to others' expectations. Even if that means they need to cheat in order to do so."[24] Kids feel so much pressure from the word "smart" that they feel they have to cheat to live up to the unrealistic expectations. They might feel dumb if they don't get the right answer. This is a big problem for our future and needs to be corrected. Just because a kid doesn't know the answer to a specific question doesn't mean he/she is unintelligent. And if that same kid happens to know the answer, it doesn't mean they are smarter than everyone else. We've accidentally tricked our students into believing this awful lie. Now, how do we correct it?

Teaching kids to relish and value their mistakes is where the real growth will happen, both personal and community growth. The mindset shift may seem subtle, but the payoff is a more caring and intelligent society. If kids no longer look at one another as competition to be devoured and instead look to one another for help and growth, what heights can we reach as a community? If adults keep this same mindset into adulthood, what can we accomplish together? Could we tackle heated political issues? Could we love our neighbor better? Could we love our families better? Yes to all three. The possibilities could be endless. It reminds me of the old Proverb that says, "If you want to go fast, go alone. *If you want to go far, go with others.*"[25] Learn to drop the smart talk and teach your peers how to fail in their favor. Go far together and enjoy the ride.

Chapter Nine

RISING TO NEW LEVELS

"It may seem difficult at first, but everything is difficult at first."

- Miyamoto Musashi

We've all hit a wall at some point in our lives. Not a physical wall, although I'm sure many people have had that experience as well. The proverbial wall I'm referring to represents the next potential chapter in our lives; it blocks our pathway and stands between us and becoming better mentally or physically. It doesn't matter what you do or where you've come from, we've all been there. *It's the moment where you ask yourself if you have what it takes to get past what's in front of you–if you're smart enough, strong enough, or if it's even worth the effort.* I think it's very important to understand that you don't have to go at it alone. There are some battles in life that you may have to fight alone, but the more you can leverage the wisdom, inspiration, and energy of those around you, the better off you will be. Allowing others around you to provide motivation and encouragement is the best way to get over that wall. Can you do it alone? Yes, no doubt. People do it and conquer their own obstacles in many individual ways. But it's so much better (and sometimes easier) to go at it with friends and family around you, people that can share not only in your wins but also help you learn from your mistakes and failures along the way.

When you come to a wall in your life, you have to possess or gain the skills and strength needed to conquer it. You might not currently possess what's needed, but that's part of the fun. That's where personal decisions come into play. You have two simple choices: You can stay where you are, or you can decide to acquire what's needed to move forward. It's not easy and never will be. It takes mental strength, consistency, and determination to push through those barricades in front of you. If you decide to acquire the needed skills, you will eventually overcome those roadblocks. The wall that once seemed improbable or impossible to conquer is now within your ability. Once you do cross over (or under), the next similar wall becomes easier. That's because you now possess the skills needed to overcome such massive hardships. Each wall has its own puzzle, but once you understand how to scale it, it's not the same problem for you as it was in the beginning. When you come to a larger, more intimidating hurdle than before, the decisions and process repeat. You once again are required to build more skills and obtain more knowledge to overcome. You can use your previous knowledge and experiences to conquer these next steps, but you must improve your techniques. The process plays itself out over and over throughout our lives. Each individual has a choice of how far she wants to go.

Take for example a carpenter. The first time he sets out to create a piece from wood, he may make something relatively small, like a wooden coaster. The carpenter may have never used a chop saw or sander before, but after gaining experience and creating a few small coasters, he now has a desire to build a step stool. He's never made a step stool before, so he has a decision to make. The new carpenter must decide if he holds the capacity to learn how to use a table saw and band saw. Once he acquires the skills to use the necessary equipment, he then can complete his new project. As he expands his skill base, the possibilities of projects compound, and the options become almost limitless. This process repeats itself in all areas of life. From music to sports and walking to running, we are intelligent, skill-based creatures. We were created to excel and level up in life. How and when we level up is the question we are trying to answer.

Another amazing part of the journey is learning to cross over difficult walls and then teaching and assisting others to cross their walls before them. After conquering your own challenges, you now have the experience you can share with others, to the benefit of others. It's gratifying and highly motivating when you are able to advise and assist others to push through their own obstacles. You encourage them to visualize themselves in a positive and empowering way, a way they might not have seen before. A situation that they thought impossible, now seems possible. These beliefs and motivations are powerful for you and the person you're encouraging. With this mindset and confidence, people are motivated to take action. Action is where the magic happens.

A destructive mindset I've experienced is that helping others makes one weak. People in power won't often admit it, but when they share helpful information with someone, they feel deep down as though they are losing power. They believe they are losing the unique ability to know more than others in some important areas. This is a false and harmful mentality to all those in their midst. There is absolutely no weakness in helping others succeed. In fact, there is strength. When you help others, you often gain additional knowledge and skills that you wouldn't have had otherwise, more wisdom than you can compound with your own. It's once again a win-win for all those involved. Help others along the way and propel yourself further than you could have alone.

The ultimate goal is not to sprint as fast as you can over every wall, but to take the time to enjoy the view. The journey of learning is the fun part. The success of overcoming your barriers is the byproduct of your journey. Beyond yourself, take time to see if anyone else is asking for help along the way. Again, it's purposeful and enjoyable to share this journey with others. This is why we have friends, why we get married, and shows the importance of family. Who you have in your inner circle really does affect how you think, what action you take, and how you feel. Choose wisely. These are the people we get to experience the highs and lows of life with. These are the people that hold your hand when you're down and hold your trophies when you're winning. These same people are not perfect but grow together with you. Not everyone experiences growth at the same time, but encouragement and support are what's needed. Not having other people to share the journey with is like being color blind. You can still see and accomplish what's needed, but life is so much more enjoyable in color.

DEFINING SUCCESS

What does it really mean to be successful? Is it about money, time, or accomplishment? Are any of those things inherently bad if stewarded correctly? Is success defined by one category? There are many billionaire savants when it comes to money, but they are sorely failing with relationships. This makes them successful in some people's eyes, but unsuccessful in areas that may matter most. How do we navigate the waters of success? First we need to clearly define what we're talking about.

From Merriam-Webster's dictionary, here's the definition of success:

Success:

n. The achievement of something desired, planned, or attempted.

n. The gaining of fame or prosperity.

If being successful means the achievement of something attempted, then that means we can still be a success, even with failures. *Does being successful depend on what others see?* I would emphatically say no! Does success improve self-confidence? Absolutely! If you nurture a growth mindset and begin to lean into your failures and the teachings of others, your success in what you pursue will be planted. It will start as that underground seed. People might not know that seed exists, but you're sprouting roots that will keep you grounded and feed your future. If you want to be successful, define what you see as successful and set small goals to get there. Whether it be money, relationships, or time, figure out what drives you. It may be a little bit of everything, and that's perfectly fine. Balance is a good thing. Once established, consistently pursue what you desire to accomplish, and you will see the fruits of your success. Learning from failures will only accelerate that growth and multiply your fruits.

Whatever your definition of success might be, I would challenge you to see success as something that should be shared–not just with your spouse or family, but with your neighbors and friends. Share your experiences and lessons. Share your time and resources. This not only helps you stay humble, but more importantly it motivates others to pursue their own successes in life. When multiple people share in a success, it multiplies the joy and impact that is created from one accomplishment. I'm not a math wizard, but I do know that multiplication is far more powerful than addition.

MALLEABLE GOALS

You never want to view yourself or others as a failure. It's hurtful to others and especially you. After all, it was Descartes that said, *"I think, therefore I am."*[26] When it comes to goals specifically, you don't want to constantly carry the feeling of being a failure around with you. Too many people set goals, and when they don't reach them, they count it as a failure. Learning to live with temporary failure and how to view it as positive is a very important skill to learn in this life. Just because you set a goal and don't meet it doesn't mean you haven't improved along the way. The goal may be aggressive and very tough to attain, but that's the point in my mind. A goal needs to push you towards action. A goal that doesn't inspire you to action is meaningless. Set goals that inspire you, but don't forget that reaching them is not what defines failure or success.

A friend asked me recently about the goals I set for myself. I told her that I set numerous goals and most of them are small, daily goals that can be tallied at the end of the year. Specifically, I told her that I had set a reachable goal of reading 5,475 pages of books last year, which comes out to fifteen pages per day. I wound up missing my goal by about 1,000 pages. She asked me if I felt like a failure? My simple and quick answer was no. I explained that I had read over 4,000 pages last year and learned new information and knowledge that I didn't have before. Even though I missed my mark, I didn't consider it failing. The goal was a beacon, guiding me in the direction I wanted to go, and the goal was not just a pass or fail number.

Your goals should guide you in life, not define you. I've discovered that the key with setting goals is to not view them as a destination. Unlike when you're traveling somewhere, you usually set a final destination. If you plan a vacation in Colorado and you only make it to Oklahoma, you will most likely be disappointed. Your skiing and mountain dinner plans can't happen in Oklahoma. It makes sense that you need the final destination for the vacation to meet expectations. On the contrary, instead of viewing your goals as a destination, like you would on a vacation, think of them as the rudder to your ship. A rudder is an underwater blade that steers the vessel, and without a rudder, a ship would simply float in random directions. Your goals help steer you in the right direction. They allow you to focus on the journey, rather than the end result. This guards you against the numbing disappointment of not reaching your goals.

Goals are great tools, and I do believe that everyone should set them. Personal goals, family goals, and business goals–setting goals allows your mind to focus on your tasks (small and large) and set you on the course for your success. It might not be a bad idea to buy a small toy ship to place in your office or home as a reminder of where you're headed. When you see this ship, remind yourself that your goals are in place to steer you in the direction you desire to go.

One of my favorite times of the year is when my wife and I set aside time to talk about the upcoming year and the goals we're striving for. We get to talk through our personal goals, as well as goals for our marriage and goals we would love to achieve together. That time also allows us to review past goals and either celebrate or laugh together at what we've reached for in the past. Nothing is off limits. We can review and talk about anything and everything. It allows our internal rudders to realign and hopefully point in the same direction again. It's easy for anyone to veer off course during the year, and it's crucial to have someone on your side to lovingly get you back on track.

Your goals should also be flexible and revisable. Just because they're on paper doesn't mean you can't revise them. Your goals should be malleable. Malleable can be defined as, "being easily controlled or influenced."[27] I'm not advocating that you change your goals daily or hourly, as that could lead to insanity and inaction, but rather allow your goals to be formed and shaped through wise counsel and meaningful conversation. There is another definition of malleable. The definition that I'm referring to is, "capable of being shaped or formed, as by hammering or pressure." When you set a goal, it doesn't need to be set in stone. Instead allow the experience of yourself and others to shape that goal, possibly into something better.

My dream and goal as a young boy was to play professional baseball. I set goals and created disciplines to become the best player I could be in order to achieve my dream. Long story short, my childhood dream never materialized and the day I knew my playing days were over was an emotionally intense day for me. Looking back, I see how my goal of becoming a professional baseball player was not my only rudder. I wanted to be a great teammate, possess great character, and be a positive influence on those around me. Even though my goal of playing professionally never transpired, the other skills I had been working on at the same time transferred seamlessly to life after baseball. Some may see me as a failure because I never played in the big leagues but I would disagree. My dream guided me to be better in so many areas, not just baseball. Once my professional dream was no longer alive, it was time to pivot my focus and discipline into new areas.

Allow yourself to redirect your rudder and point you in a slightly new direction. If you need to add to your goal, do it. If you need to take away from your goal, do that in order to get yourself back on track. Allow yourself grace, and never view yourself as a failure. Goal setting is an art and shouldn't be a prison sentence. Goals should lead you to your better self and not discourage you from reaching your full potential.

ADDING TO YOUR ENGINE

What you allow into your mind and body can make a big difference. If you fill your body with junk food then consequently, you may be low on energy and overweight. If you fill your mind with negative thoughts and surround yourself with negative people, then you'll probably have a negative outlook on any event that happens in your life. On the other hand, if you nourish your body with nutritious food, you may enjoy the benefits of more energy and less guilt. Fill your mind with wisdom from books and surround yourself with positive people and you will reap the benefits. What you add to your engine makes all the difference in the world. Be very aware of the internal investments you make in yourself.

Consider nitrous oxide (N_2O) and its potential. Nitrous oxide is used as a fuel injector in gas engines to get more performance and power out of vehicles. When you heat nitrous oxide to 570° Fahrenheit, it splits into oxygen and nitrogen. This means that there is now more oxygen in your engine, which allows for more fuel to be injected, which in turn allows the vehicle to go much faster. The exact same engine can produce more power, simply by adding N_2O. Nothing else has changed in the engine, just the substance injected into the engine.[28] Learning from mistakes can be the nitrous oxide to your brain. Eating the right nutrition and only allowing positive thoughts into your mind can be your N_2O. You can be the same person, but with the correct additive and mindset, you can produce more energy and wisdom than you thought possible. Simply being conscious of the drastic difference in output is a great place to start. Once you begin to see the difference, you won't want to go back to the way it was before.

Nitrous oxide can also have a downside. It is very bulky, takes up a lot of space, and the engine needs a lot of it to perform; therefore, you can only carry a certain amount of N_2O on board. The driver usually has a button to inject N_2O and uses it at opportune times to increase performance. You can't constantly use it, because there is a limited supply. Just as nitrous oxide can be bulky, you need to be aware of the amount of failure that's entering your life. Too much failure can be overwhelming and take a toll on your mental and physical stability. The goal is not to fail, the goal is to learn from your failures and the failures of others. The correct amount of temporary failure in your life is different for each individual, but it can have a negative effect if not properly balanced. Be aware of how you or your loved ones are reacting to failure. If it's weighing heavy on you, back off until you feel mentally ready to conquer more lessons. Failure is a powerful tool, but a tool can also do harm. Learn to use this tool in the correct way, so you can use failure to its fullest and greatest potential.

Think of it another way. You don't have to change your engine or wish to be a different person in order to reach your full potential. Adding the right mindset for navigating failures will produce a significant boost to your own engine, your brain. With a new failure forward mindset, your same engine can run more efficiently and produce more power. No need to wish you were smarter or more intelligent, because you have all you need right now. Just change the input in order to change the output. Let failures be the propellant that adds that extra boost to your internal drive. You don't need to be anyone else, as you are perfectly built to be great exactly as you are.

Not many people see the catalyst of using failures to propel you forward even faster. Most people just want to gloat about their successes, but it's the lessons learned that brought that success. The key is to open your eyes and cleanse your mind. Be fully aware that nearly everyone you meet has the ability to be your teacher. You can learn from literally anyone. An anonymous source once said, *"Everything and everyone is your teacher unless you are a bad student."* Don't be a bad student. Pay attention. Those overlooked lessons from failures can and will be a catalyst for your success.

POWER TO SPARE

When you're filling your mind with wisdom and taking care of your body, you will begin to notice a surplus. This surplus is built up with consistency over the course of weeks and months. As you grow, it grows. That extra bit of knowledge and energy you can give the right person at the right moment is what you're aiming for. That surplus you're able to pass along can carry over to their lives and affect them in a great and meaningful way. She doesn't have to be like-minded, and he doesn't have to see the world as you do. You just need to possess the extra capacity in order to share what you know or give him the attention he needs. Sometimes you won't even notice what you're doing, but it makes a difference. More and more people will want to be around you because you lift them up and encourage them. You will become a resource that people look forward to speaking with. When you have and share a surplus, you will empower others.

Empowering others is vital to your success, in my opinion. Having and drawing from a surplus of wisdom and energy is the only way to do it. The energy you give to others, just like the giving of money, will come back to you tenfold–there's no doubt in my mind about this. People long to be around a person that motivates them. A person that makes them feel like they can take on their day and get through rough patches with confidence. With this sharing of your surplus will come more opportunities. You will be amazed at the doors that will open up to you and the doors that thankfully close. Opportunities, and the ability to say yes or no to those opportunities, are where you take your next step. Remember, you're not searching for money, but ultimately you're on the prowl for wisdom. When you build up your supply of wisdom and energy, share it with others. You will get a return, just like an investment, unlike anything you've ever imagined.

CONSUMED BY WISDOM, NOT MONEY

I recently read the book *Think and Grow Rich* by Napoleon Hill[29], and it impacted me in a way I didn't expect. As I turned the pages and digested the content, I realized that what we habitually think about becomes our nature. It can become an all-consuming fire–to the point that it can be dangerous. For example, if you wake up in the morning and declare your affirmation of making twenty million dollars, that will become your priority. It will consume your thoughts and actions. Making that twenty million dollars will take precedence over anything else in your life. It doesn't matter if you have a wife, family, or friends that need your time and attention. The goal of making that money will be all that consumes you. When you're faced with a decision of spending time with a loved one or spending an extra night working, what you obsess about will win every time. Your consistent thoughts will come to fruition through your actions, and those actions have consequences. This is why it's so important to prioritize your goals and thoughts. It's exactly what Francis Bacon knew when he said, "Money is a great servant, but a terrible master."[30] Make money your tool, not the tool that uses and abuses you. Make wisdom and time your focus and allow the money to fall where it may. Let me be perfectly clear–there's nothing wrong with making money. Make as much money as you can handle and steward it wisely. God blesses those who give, and the kingdom needs financial backing. But when you place making money above all else, it will often cause more harm than good. Your closest relationships often suffer the most harm.

As I continued through Hill's book, I wondered what would happen if I chose to focus on something other than money. If growing rich is as simple as thinking about such and daily affirmations, then shouldn't the path to wisdom be just as simple? Another book called *The Richest Man in Babylon* teaches how to focus on accruing wisdom and not money. Focus on the right thing, and the money will follow. What if I started with the lesson from The Richest Man in Babylon and applied it along with the lesson from *Think and Grow Rich*? *The Richest Man in Babylon* is a short but powerful story. It tells the tale of a young man seeking to build his fortune. He crosses paths with an older, wiser man who teaches him to not seek riches but instead wisdom. The old man teaches the young man that wisdom is the foundation of true riches and wealth.[31]

If wealth is a by-product of wisdom like it teaches in *The Richest Man in Babylon*, then what reason do we have to chase wealth? Many thoughts came to my mind regarding this. What good does making endless amounts of money do a person in the end? Money can easily be passed down to the next generation, but it will be gone rather quickly if they don't know how to steward that wealth. What if I shifted my focus? What if I began to contemplate and collect as much wisdom as possible? It seems clear to me now: the main focus for me going forward is to grow in wisdom, not financial status. The wealth follows the know-how. And instead of keeping wisdom to myself, if someone were to ask, I would be open to sharing anything I know. Not a know-it-all, but a resource for others when needed. The only way to achieve this goal was to focus my attention and energy on gaining wisdom. For me, that meant consistently looking for opportunities and praying for wisdom. It is by no means a get-rich-quick scheme, but takes patience and a confident eye towards the future.

Many other writings, including the Bible, teach on the subject of wisdom. Proverb states, *"Let the wise hear and increase in learning, and the one who understands obtain guidance."* (Proverbs 1:5)[32] God designed and gave us an intelligent brain for a reason. I believe that He wants us to grow, learn, and ultimately share. He calls us to encourage others and not selfishly hold on to our money or wisdom for our own selfish gain.

Let's look again at the parable referenced earlier in Matthew 25 about the evil servant who buried his money from a different perspective. I love learning and teaching from parables because the stories can have numerous takeaways for many different people. Each person that listens with a unique perspective might be able to derive a slightly different meaning–it's like an abstract painting. When we set a goal to experience this story from a slightly different perspective, we can begin to ask questions–and good questions lead to great conversations. What if Jesus (who told the parable) was speaking not about gold, but wisdom? What if He was trying to tell us that the real gold is in the wisdom we share and put to work? That wisdom and the unprotected sharing of truth is the key? Wisdom contains the power to dethrone kings, stop wars, and crumble corrupt empires.

It could be a stretch, but I fully believe it's a perspective worth thinking about. Most unique perspectives are worth investigating. When you gain knowledge from a mentor or peer, the best thing you can do is pass it along to someone else who is willing to listen. Once you possess knowledge and wisdom, don't hide away and keep it to yourself–it's designed to be shared.

If you allow money to be your rudder in life, you will have issues at some point in your journey–as it will fall apart when you need it most. Instead, commission wisdom to be your rudder. Fill your thoughts with truth and when you need it most, truth will come through for you. After all, it is truth that sets you free.

Chapter Ten

LEARNING
FROM PAIN

"I can bear any pain
as long as it has meaning."

- Haruki Murakami

Pain can be a great teacher if we're paying attention. Although pain can be rough at times, there is value in your painful experiences. Pain can be a signal that you need to change or that you're already changing. Do all you can to never waste the opportunity. It could be physical pain from touching a hot stove or emotional pain from saying an unkind word to a friend. You can learn a lot from your pain and the pain of others. Instead of viewing pain as an inconvenience and always trying to avoid it, why not view it as another vehicle for learning? We naturally try to avoid pain, which isn't necessarily a bad thing for our survival. We don't want our lives to be in a constant state of pain, but when pain does make itself known, we need to do our best to listen to what it's trying to teach us.

Oftentimes the physical pain we feel in our body is actually our body telling us that something isn't right. Instead of numbing the pain with drugs that only cover up the problem, we can instead listen to the pain and try to get to the root of the problem. Avoiding the pain doesn't offer any sort of solution, but only allows the pain to manifest below the surface. When pain is not dealt with, it can leak into other areas of your life. If you're hurting from a headache, you may be more likely to lash out at your spouse or friends if they're not aware of your situation. If you allow stress to build up from work or life, without properly disposing of that stress, it can lead to serious health problems and even cancer. Suppressed pain can be a cancer, both physically and mentally. Deal with the pain now, do your best to learn from the pain, and move past the pain as gracefully and consciously as you can.

Learning from pain can also produce humility. Your painful experience can make you a stronger person and give you invaluable insights into your strengths and weaknesses–strengths that you can learn to lean into and weaknesses you can improve. Pain can also allow you to connect on a deeper level with others that have gone through a similar experience. It's nearly impossible to fully understand what someone else is going through if you have not gone through something similar. It's very difficult to empathize with friends if you haven't experienced the pain they are sorting through. When you share such a deep connection with another person through the lens of a painful experience, you can help her through her current situation and see her to the other side. Even when you don't see what can possibly be learned from your painful situation, there can be a benefit to helping a friend or stranger at a later time.

You may see now that pain can not only help you move forward and become a better person, but your pain can also benefit other people in a positive way for both parties. Physical and mental pain is not something to be wished for, but if we can lean into it, the learning mindset can make it a little more bearable.

LEARNING AND GROWING IS UNCOMFORTABLE

I recently watched a short video of Navy Seals training in action. There were about ten men, all linked by arms, standing on the beach. Their instructor would order them to get down on the ground, and they would have to all lay down on their backs with their arms still linked. No sooner than they were down, they were ordered to stand up together. This happened again and again and again. This was clearly not their first exercise for the day, as they were covered in sand and had looks of agony and pain on their faces. Just the act of standing up was hard at this point. As they continued the exercise, the stronger men helped adjust for the ones that were lagging behind. Two men in the human chain would use what strength they had left to pull another up who was struggling. The man who was struggling was trying, but he was exhausted–*both physically and mentally*. By the end of the exercise, the group of men was working in unison and sharing in the pain that others felt. I'm sure the sand ground into their flesh and caused severe rashing, making it even more difficult and ten times more painful. Towards the end, it seemed that the trainees' bodies were close to shutting down on them. But they all managed to get through it together. The men needed each other. At the end of the exercise, the instructor said, "Where there is discomfort, there is growth."[33] Read that again and commit it to memory. Always remember that phrase when you feel discomfort or discouragement while learning something new or training. There is always room for growth. There is always something that you could improve. This honestly keeps life exciting. The available room for growth shouldn't be a burden but a blessing. Sometimes life can be a grind, but that's not an excuse to close your eyes and act like it's not happening. Link arms with someone that encourages and motivates you and carry on. You'll be better for it.

BAD THINGS CAN BE FUEL

I've learned over the years that sometimes bad things just suck and there's no other way around it. It can be hard to see past the difficult moment, but if you can, there's fuel to be had. When you set your mind to see the positive in any situation, you program yourself to be prepared. Prepared for good things to come from the bad. That doesn't mean you go out looking for something bad to fuel you, but when it comes along, you react according to your preparedness. When people go through difficult situations with a smile and positive attitude, it can change peoples' lives. The pain is transformed into positive energy and lessons to be learned. It's very difficult and that's why so few people are able to do it.

Hal Elrod is an amazing example of using pain as fuel. He suffered a car wreck as a young man, and it almost killed him. At first the doctors said he probably wouldn't survive. A week after his accident, they thought he would never come out of the vegetative state. When he was finally discharged, he was sent home with the conclusion that he would never walk again. He shocked the doctors and nurses with how positive he was throughout the entire process. They actually thought he was mentally ill because of the continuously positive mindset he possessed. He went on to perfect and write *The Miracle Morning*. *The Miracle Morning* is a daily routine that can lead to incredible results. It brings physical activity, wisdom, and peace in a consistent way into your life. If you haven't read the book or heard his story, it's definitely worth your time.[34]

Why do I bring up this example? Because examples like this change thought patterns on how a person learns from painful situations, especially during the moment. If you have your mind right, you can take notes, consciously ponder, and learn from any situation, good or bad. Just because you've been dealt a crappy hand doesn't mean you won't soon get a new one. Working through tough times is an art and takes grace and understanding.

Another aspect of bad things being fuel is the interaction with negative people. It's often easy to be fueled by people who encourage and support you, but what happens when you're confronted with negativity? I would confidently say that you can still use this. If you're grounded and confident in who you are and your ability to think on your own, you can use negativity as fuel. I did this in high school when coaches and other players said I was too small or too slow to play Division I baseball. It drove me to practice more and be more intentional with what I learned. When scouts overlooked me or talked down to me, it motivated me. It truthfully hurt and annoyed me as well, but it mostly motivated me to prove them wrong. I turned their negativity into a positive outcome for me. Just because someone says a negative word about you doesn't mean that they have the final say. That's only one thought in a sea of opinions. You have the final say with how you respond, how you act, and how you treat yourself going forward. You have to believe in yourself first before anyone else will.

Consider these examples: if people attack your intelligence and demean you for not thinking as they do, use that as fuel to study and learn on your own. If you have a question, ask confidently and follow where it leads, no matter the chatter or outcome. If others call you fat, use that as motivation to eat healthier, go help someone else in a similar situation, or start a workout program. Or if you're comfortable with where you're at, forgive them and let it be. People are entitled to their own opinion, but it's not always right. If people say you'll never be able to start a business, ask why they think that way and learn from your shortcomings. Everyone has weaknesses and learning what your weaknesses are can be a blessing. Your mindset of how you process incoming negative information is key to everything. Process it correctly, and it turns to fuel–fuel that you can use for yourself and positively impact others.

THE NARROW PATH

Success and consistency are not easy. They never will be. Like my dad always told me growing up, *"If it was easy, everyone would do it."* Just because something isn't easy doesn't mean it's the right or wrong thing to do, but it can be an indicator. The Bible touches on this when it talks about taking the narrow path concerning our morals:

"Enter through the narrow gate. For wide is the gate and broad is the road that leads to destruction, and many enter through it. But small is the gate and narrow the road that leads to life, and only a few find it." (Matthew 7:13-14).

I would strongly claim those verses can be applied to business and success as well. Do you choose the seemingly difficult, narrow path to future success, or do you choose the easy path that most likely leads to little or no personal success? If you choose the narrow path, you're trading short-term pain for long-term gain. If you choose the broad, easy path, you're trading short-term ease for not much of anything in the long term.

If you can wrap your head around seeking difficult things to carry out and learn from, it will make those hard seasons in your life take on much more meaning. Look beyond the easy that's right in front of you and shift your focus to long-term gains. It will make learning and humility come a little easier. When you're confused about a certain subject you're reading, take that as a sign you're learning something new. Your brain is confused because it's trying to piece connections together in your mind. It's the same as when you lift weights at the gym. When it's hard to lift and you're struggling through your last rep, your body is in intense pain. That beautiful pain, when applied correctly, is what you're seeking. The old adage, "pain is gain", is pretty accurate. Seek that same pain and confusion when learning. When you get frustrated that you don't understand a new concept, lean into that and push through. Read it four times if you have to, or put it together ten times until you understand. Even if you don't understand it completely, your brain is fusing that new information into your sub-conscious for another day. Your brain is more powerful than you will ever know. Remember, pain is gain in the brain. Your willingness to sacrifice short-term pain and confusion for long-term gains is what will define your level of success.

Another great piece of wisdom someone shared with me recently is to judge your progress by your lows and not your highs. You will always have ups and downs, no matter what you do. If you are always basing your progress on your highs, you will have the chance of becoming more erratic and emotionally unstable. Getting discouraged or distracted is easy when you're bouncing from one big high to one crushing low. High one day, down the next. Instead, focus on working on your weaknesses and low points. If you can become incrementally better in one of your weak areas, that will compound into your overall growth. Your strengths will still be there *(you can still work on them as well)* and your highs and lows will start to balance out. Higher lows and higher highs should work in unison and not like opposing magnets. Keep this in mind when you're learning new things.

Chapter Eleven

OVERFLOW MENTALITY

"Yesterday I was clever, so I wanted to
change the world. Today I am wise,
so I am changing myself."

- Rumi

If your cup is empty, it's hard to share water with someone else. You need your cup to be full and even overflowing in order to have the ability to share with others. The question is how do we get there? There are several ways to reach an abundant, overflow mentality including filling your mind up with positive messages, surrounding yourself with people that lift you up, or simply by giving.

THE RULE OF GIVING

Giving is an amazingly simple way to learn humility and gratitude. Some might argue that it's the only way. When you give, you tend to notice the impact it has on the recipient. You're fully aware of the relief, surprise, or simple joy that a gift brings. Did you also know that giving can have a positive effect on your health? According to the Cleveland Clinic, giving of your time or money can lead to lower blood pressure, increased self-esteem, lower stress, and a longer, happier life. Biologically speaking, giving can activate pleasure regions in the brain, which release dopamine, serotonin, and oxytocin. You can literally become addicted to giving and be better for it.[35] If you're going to be addicted to something, that something might as well bring others joy and better yourself. Giving is a win-win.

There's also another aspect of giving that is often overlooked. The giving of knowledge. When you share knowledge, not only do you feel good about yourself, but you directly impact another person's life–you help them become a better person. Whether it's knowledge of how to change a diaper or how to make a million dollars, if someone is willing to listen and learn, the sharing of knowledge benefits both parties.

THE IMPORTANCE OF SELF-ESTEEM

Have you ever done something that someone else has criticized you for? How did that make you feel? Were you able to overcome that situation or does it still affect you to this day? The importance of self-esteem in this path to better yourself can not be understated. You need a courageous and unwavering self-confidence that will carry you through the rough waters of learning from failures. There will be doubt and ridicule from others, along with your own. Unwavering self-esteem will help balance out the ups and downs and provide a massive impact on the direction of your choices and growth.

How do you go about obtaining high self-esteem? I don't believe it's found in yourself. You are imperfect and will always be imperfect, therefore you need to look outside yourself for purpose and worth. If you base your self-esteem on your actions alone, you will often let yourself down. When you look outside yourself and up to a higher power, you have an unwavering stream of love and purpose that fills your self-confidence. Once filled, you can then pass along this confidence to others. However, not just any god will do. I believe the only true god that can give this unwavering self-confidence is the God of the Bible. When you tap into the power that God gives, your opportunities can be limitless. Filling up with power from Yahweh allows you

153

to build true self-esteem and selflessly build others up along the way.

If you have high and consistent self-esteem, you're able to keep a favorable view of yourself, even when you make a mistake. This gives you the freedom to make mistakes without viewing yourself as a failure. The temporary failure can be viewed not as an end, but a transition between successes. Without that freedom, you may not even try for fear of looking like a failure to yourself and others. If you can't have a positive view of yourself after a misstep, how can you expect others to? They simply won't. Respect from others, in any scenario, begins and ends with you. You can control the amount of respect others have for you by leading the way and setting the example. Set an example by taking responsibility for your actions. That means owning up to your mistakes and not blaming others. It's very easy to shift the blame to a third party when things go wrong. But a person with high self-esteem accepts responsibility when it's not convenient to do so.

I've been fortunate to be taught the importance of self-esteem through the words and actions of family and mentors. What I had learned showed itself in a situation in college. It was my sophomore year, and I had a paper to write. It wasn't a long paper, it only had to be two or three pages, if I remember correctly. I played collegiate baseball and lived with most of my teammates in three dorm rooms on campus. We all left the doors to our rooms open and trusted the entire team. Most guys would go in and out of each other's rooms and not think twice about it. One afternoon, I finished the paper and left the document open on my laptop, which did not have a password at the time. The time came to turn in the paper and I did so, knowing I completed the assignment. About a week later, the teacher asked me to stay after class and called me into his office. I was astonished when he told me that I had plagiarized my paper. It was nearly a word-for-word copy from someone else in the class. I asked who it was and when I discovered the culprit, I knew what had happened. He told me that he was going to have to give me a zero for the assignment and that he was very disappointed in me.

I then had a choice to make. Do I rage against my teammate and throw a fit because this clearly isn't fair? Because in all reality, it wasn't fair. It was far from fair. Or do I accept the outcome and figure out how to make up for it? I am confident that the self-esteem I acquired over the first nineteen years of my life had a lot to do with my decision. I chose the latter path. Since I had no evidence that my paper was the original, I told my teacher that I would accept the zero under one circumstance. He had to know that I did not cheat and plagiarize that paper. That's not who I am. I then asked how I could make up the lost points from the paper, as it was a decent chunk of our grade in the class. He allowed me to join him on a Saturday and help clean out a storage facility full of old school equipment for bonus points. I think I actually received more bonus points from that Saturday than the paper was worth. I also finished the class on a high note and gained respect from the teacher.

Again, I am confident that I was able to make this decision because of the high self-esteem that I carried. Even if the teacher would have called me a cheater and not allowed me to make up the points, I would have known the truth. The truth is more important than what other people think is the truth. Especially when it comes to yourself. I still remember the conversation and sitting in his office to this day. Things like that stick with you for good. That experience is such a great reminder for me. Even when it's not your fault, sometimes you get dealt a hand that you must play. It's a little easier to play a bad hand when you have self-confidence as a part of your foundation. Going forward, try to see those situations as opportunities to improve.

When you display high and consistent self-esteem, you also encourage others in the process. Your abundance of self-confidence will spill over into other lives. High self-esteem is not about putting yourself first and others second, it's about sharing the confidence that is overflowing within you. You absolutely need to be healthy yourself in order to help other people. From abundance comes wealth. And the wealth I'm currently referring to is that of confidence.

THE GIFT OF BEING PRESENT

When you are present in a conversation, you are not only giving a gift to your counterpart, you are also giving a gift to yourself. The gifts of being present include boosting creativity, improving relationships, and reducing stress. Fully engaging in a conversation will allow the stresses of yesterday and tomorrow to melt from your mind. It allows you to focus on the present. Being fully focused on the present moment means more of what you experience stays with you. It's not a fleeting moment but a lasting impression.

Being present is definitely something I need to work on, and my wife would agree. During a conversation with Kendra, it's very easy to be thinking of the next project or what I have to do tomorrow, but when I do this, it robs her of value. Even if it's something simple, like trying to remember if I took the trash out, it signals to my wife that the task I'm contemplating is more important than her. I want to add value to her life, not take it away. Even though making her feel unimportant is the farthest thing from my intentions, that is how it comes across. If I'm aware of what I'm doing in a conversation, I'm more likely to take the necessary steps to correct what's needed.

A big key to being present in a conversation is eye contact. With eye contact, you're engaging and signaling to your counterpart that you're ready to fully interact. Without eye contact, it's easy to come across as uninterested or annoyed, which doesn't set the stage for a good conversation. Another key factor in being present is body language. Leaning forward, good posture, and facing your discussion partner says a lot without having to use words. It's all about setting the stage for someone to open up in a conversation. If a person feels like you're interested and engaged, they're more likely to have a meaningful conversation. Even if you're not involved in a conversation, you can still practice being present by using your amazing God-given senses to experience your setting. Focusing on the sounds, smells, or sights can help draw you into being present and fully experiencing each moment.

Again, I can't stress enough how much value being present gives to others. It's crucial for you to come from a humble state of mind and a desire to know more about the situation or person you're engaging with. Being present makes people feel valued and appreciated. And the skill of being present translates to every area of your life. The more you focus on being present, the faster your desired growth will be. The more you're able to be present in the moment, the more you're able to filter and learn in those moments.

When I was in school, I often daydreamed and did not pay attention in class. I was thinking of the next basketball game at recess or what I was going to do after school. I was not engaged and was rather bored. I knew that I had to do well in school in order to play sports, so I figured out how to make this work. What I discovered was when I paid attention to the lesson at hand, I actually could retain information. I didn't have to cram at the last minute for a test and actually reduced the amount of time that I had to engage with school. If I just listened intently and did my best to be present, I could skip the all-nighter study sessions and get a good night's sleep. This also gave me more time to play sports or hang out with friends. It wasn't always easy, but it worked really well for me.

Being present is also a trade-off, but it's well worth it. When we started creating passive income and started our design business, most of the work was front-loaded. We knew it was going to be difficult at the beginning, but we did the work anyway. We were present and focused through the hard part. As time went on, the work lessened and the passive income stayed steady. The work and income seemed to get a little easier as our work and progress compounded. Being present is similar. It's not easy to fully engage and be present in the moment. It takes practice, practice, and more practice. But the more you can be present in the moment, the more you're able to retain later. The little details you're able to recall in future conversations and the rate at which you grow will start to compound. Your friends and loved ones will notice and thank you. You will give them tremendous value rather than taking it away.

Being present is a game-changer. It's actually life-changing. In *The Power of Habit*, Charles Duhigg speaks about keystone habits. A keystone habit is one that is closely tied to other good habits.[36] Developing one keystone habit can lead to the rapid development of other good habits. I believe being present is a keystone habit. It takes work, but if you can get in the routine of being present, you'll see many other positive results come directly from this base habit. Set this as a foundation and build your other habits off this wide base. The value that being present brings to you and others is worth the trade-off of focus and energy. Being present is a short-term tradeoff with a long-term payoff.

Chapter Twelve

FAILING
IN STYLE

"Success is not final, failure is not fatal: it is
the courage to continue that counts."

- Winston Churchill

It can be a touchy subject, but there's no doubt in my mind that the public school system is failing students. Not the teachers, but the system. I, myself, am a product of public schools and after going through it and studying the alternatives, I can see the fruit of what something different yields. Most schools teach us to try and be perfect. You're always aiming for that perfect score on the test or the perfect grade in the class. You are punished for your mistakes and oftentimes looked down upon when you have an incorrect answer. Students are intimidated by teachers, or other students, to give an answer in class for fear of it being wrong.

I remember in high school being docked points because I didn't show my work the correct way on a math test. I got the right answer, but I didn't arrive at the correct answer the way the teacher wanted me to. I understand that she was trying to teach a formula, but the fact that I arrived at the answer from a different path, and that path was denied for no good reason, was interesting to me. I didn't realize it at the time, because I was very frustrated, but it was a great lesson in the end. Sometimes there are many paths to the correct answer! The focus should be the solution, not precisely how you get there.

If students are not allowed to think differently in school, then we are training robots that simply memorize and repeat answers. They don't learn to think critically on their own. Teaching kids that there can be more than one way is a great benefit to their minds and future. I really enjoyed math at the time of that testing faux pas but was soured after that. I didn't pursue math any further in college and only took what I needed to get through. I am thankful for the lesson it taught me, but this small shift changed my path.

The task of changing a decades old school system is a large undertaking. It will not and cannot happen overnight, and I don't want to complain about a problem without at least proposing a solution. Let's not forget, there are a lot of brilliant and caring teachers in the public school system, but they are often weighed down by pressure from other teachers or rules from the educational system.

We can start by encouraging children to think logically and ask questions. Often, teachers have a lesson plan they are required to follow, and questions hinder the timing and execution of that plan. Questions should be looked at as assets; no question should ever be viewed as unintelligent. Maybe we could have a blocked period in school where the only goal is to ask stupid questions. As dumb as that sounds, can you imagine the questions that would arise from middle school and high school students? Some good, some funny, and some inappropriate, but all teaching the process of asking questions in a respectful manner. If the teachers don't know an answer, the students are taught how to find answers. Even if they do know, the students are allowed to check the answers and discuss a different point of view. This would take courage and self-confidence from teachers and leaders to put themselves in that vulnerable position of not having all the answers, but in the end everyone involved would be better for it. Why would we not want students asking questions under the guidance of more knowledgeable adults instead of the alternative of asking those questions to immature classmates, which most likely will produce immature answers?

It's not just up to the school system either–parents will also need to play a role. Too many parents want to seem like they have all the answers for every situation. This is not healthy in any way as no one has all the answers. When a parent says that they know best and then a child learns that there is a different way or another "right" answer, that parent loses credibility. The child then seeks counsel and wisdom from other sources. If parents could simply admit that they don't know something and be open to working through it together, it would be a massive step in the right direction. It's not perfect, and never will be. Everyone is different and sometimes situations are out of people's control. Even with that in mind, the progress toward the goal of understanding and learning to ask questions would be well worth the effort.

MAKE A GOAL OF LOOKING STUPID

When was the last time you set out to look stupid in any given situation? It could be a conversation, how to play a game, or carrying out a simple task. If I'm guessing correctly, the answer is never. What could possibly be the point of doing this? Why would you intentionally set out to make yourself look like you don't know something? Take a moment to think about what the consequences of looking the fool could bring. First of all, as a negative, someone might think less of you in the short term. Is that something you would be willing to put up with? Would you trade a short-term result for long-term growth? And even if those people think you're foolish, how they respond after the fact says a lot about who they are. You can tell a lot about a person when you admit you don't know something. Does he make you feel even dumber by saying, "You don't know that!" in a sarcastic and demeaning tone? Or does he understand and take the time to explain the knowledge he possesses and pass it along to you? You want to be around people that encourage and foster you to be the best version of yourself you can be. Think of trying to look stupid in front of people as a life filter for those you want to be around.

When you make a point to look stupid or like you don't understand something, you open yourself up to solutions you may not have known existed. You enter a state of humility and open yourself up to learning from someone you might have thought wasn't worth learning from. If you never ask for help, how will anyone ever have the chance to show you a new way? Jordan Peterson once said, "You have to be willing to be a fool to advance." If acting a fool opens new doors and new pathways for you to learn and accelerate your growth, why not give it a try? The only thing you have to fear is what others will think of you at that moment. If you can get past that feeling of embarrassment, there's so much waiting for you on the other side.

If you learn to lay down your ego, you also learn to be real. Being real with yourself and others leads to real results and real growth, not fake growth. Ryan Holiday says it well in his book, *Ego is the Enemy*:

"When we remove ego, we're left with what is real. What replaces ego is humility, yes—but rock-hard humility and confidence. Whereas ego is artificial, this type of confidence can hold weight. Ego is stolen.

Confidence is earned. Ego is self-anointed, its swagger is artifice. One is girding yourself, the other gaslighting. It's the difference between potent and poisonous."[37]

Learn to have the freedom of looking stupid. Strive to build a rock-hard humility and confidence that doesn't break under pressure. Make the ridiculous goal of looking stupid at least once a week to start with and then add more once you get the hang of it. It doesn't have to always be some big moment, so try starting with a small task. And you don't need to physically act unintelligent, you just need to ask questions that have simple answers. Prepare to be amazed at the real, lasting fruit the simple act will bring forth. Hidden fruit that would have never been uncovered with you digging in a little deeper. Just remember that looking stupid often comes in the form of a question.

If you trade looking dumb today for adding more intelligence and knowledge for tomorrow, that's a win. Stacking small wins day after day becomes a compounding effect of knowledge. That compounding effect will lead you to things you didn't realize were possible. Learn how to learn, and the rest will take care of itself.

FAILURE FRIDAYS

If you're looking for a specific way to plug into a different mindset in order to improve, try Failure Fridays. It's a very simple concept with lasting results. The rule is this: every Friday, set a goal to perform a task you don't yet know how to do. You can double up and set a goal to read a concept or topic that you don't understand as well. Doing this weekly will shift your thinking and allow you to relax in the learning process. The learning process can be mentally draining, but when you learn to appreciate the effort it takes to learn, you become grateful for the struggle. There are so many things that you don't know how to do. That's the fun part. That's what keeps life exciting. View all these unknown skills and knowledge as a gift. If you already knew how to do everything, life would be pretty boring.

During your Failure Fridays, give yourself permission to get frustrated along the way. Learn how to deal with those frustrations of not knowing how to do something or not getting it right the first time. Lean into those emotions and learn to redirect the frustration into focus. You can use that emotional energy in a good way. When you learn something new, it can act as a drug. It can be invigorating and bring new energy to your life. It can be addicting. The biggest caution with learning new things is to not keep what you learn to yourself, but to make an effort to pass along your newly learned skill to those who ask and are willing to listen. What good is all the knowledge in the world if you can't share it with those seeking? It only leads to power trips and weak relationships. Strengthen those around you with knowledge and wisdom. The knowledge and know-how you give will come back to you in abundance.

Remember, when seeking to learn, you don't always have to learn from your own failures. That's why there are instruction manuals with complicated mechanisms. That's why people write articles and books;

they want to share the information. You'll hear a lot of people say, *"I don't want other people to make the same mistakes I did."* You can learn from someone else much more quickly than trying to build something from nothing.

When you learn from someone else's mistakes, you're still learning. You're learning at a new level, even if you don't understand it. It's actually one of the best ways to learn, and I see it as a cheat code. I loved cheat codes when I was young playing *Mario Bros.* on Nintendo. Why would the game designers include special passages to skip levels and win the game faster, if they didn't want us using them? There's nothing wrong with skipping levels–you just have to pay attention, learn as you go, and desire to get to your destination.

Give Failure Fridays a try and see what happens. What's the worst thing that could happen? More importantly, what's the best thing that could happen? I know from experience that the good outweighs the bad.

A BETTER FUTURE

Imagine a world where you could actually change the world. Not just say it, but actually take steps to do that. There's nothing wrong with thinking big, but how do you accomplish big things? You accomplish big things by completing small tasks. Small tasks that are completed repeatedly, day after day, add up to big things. They compound on one another over time and these compounding actions can make us and those around us better. If we can imagine for a moment, let's envision a world where people aren't afraid to ask questions. It doesn't matter how smart you are or where you come from, it only matters that you ask the right questions and are willing to learn. If people weren't afraid of looking unintelligent, how much could they learn? How much more could we accomplish and at what pace?

When I think of the barriers to people engaging and asking questions, it's almost as though people are speaking different languages. Obviously, when someone speaks another language you're not familiar with, it's almost impossible to understand what that person is saying. Communication halts into a slow pace or the conversation dies altogether. If we can learn to speak the language of questions, coupled with building others up, we will communicate in a way that most everyone can understand. This disarming way to communicate can lead to positive conversations and ultimately timely actions. When I think of a better future, it's full of many questions–freedom to ask questions and the freedom to answer questions truthfully and unashamedly.

Chapter Thirteen

BE A
PROFESSIONAL

"You can't be an important and life-
changing presence for some people
without also being a joke and an
embarrassment to others."

- Mark Manson

What does it take to be a professional failure? Just that phrase makes me smile. Most people will hear that and think it's negative, but it's definitely not when you understand where you're going and what you're looking for. The professional failure plays the long game. He doesn't look for an immediate success or score, but rather focuses on small actions that add up to big wins. A professional is committed. Through thick and thin, he has a plan and sticks to it. When situations get rough, he rises to the occasion and focuses on the long-term goal. It's a steady, lifetime commitment.

A professional is conscious of her habits and understands that her habits make up who she is and what she becomes. If a habit isn't producing the desired results, she pivots, adjusts, and carries on. She doesn't see anything as wasted time or failures, but rather as stepping stones to where she wants to eventually be.

A professional focuses on the process, not the temporary outcome. Just because an action doesn't produce the desired result right away, doesn't mean it won't produce the desired result later on. He understands that the process is more important than the temporary outcome, because it's the process that leads to the final outcome. He doesn't feel sorry for himself if things aren't going his way, as he knows that in time, with consistency and effort, success will be drawn to him and he won't have to chase it. A professional is confident in his actions and committed to bettering himself and those around him.

A professional takes action. As the saying by Confucius goes, *"To know and not do is to not yet know."*[38] If you know what you need to do, but don't take the steps to do it, you have not done anything to improve your situation or understanding. You are exactly like a person that doesn't know any better. Be someone who learns, understands, and then acts on that knowledge and wisdom. Life tends to favor those who take action. Life tends to favor people even more if they take action and then learn from those actions. When you take action, you learn how to react on your feet. You learn to think through any situation and are better for it. It's an amazing, compounding effect that pushes you forward and helps propel those around you forward as well. You become an inspiration and resource to other people.

Being a professional failure isn't easy, and it's not for everyone. It takes commitment, confidence, and a great cast of mentors around you. The best way to start is by starting today. Try something new and just simply listen and ask questions the next chance you get. It doesn't take much to get started, but it does take some effort.

EQUAL PLAYING FIELD

We have been given the gift of a brain that is much more powerful than most people realize. A perfectly designed brain that can solve problems, create beautiful artwork, and store massive amounts of information. While physical and mental disabilities exist, the vast majority of people start on the same playing field. While our external circumstances differ greatly, our internal make-up and unlimited potential start the same. In America, this comes with personal responsibility and freedom–a personal responsibility that most people choose to not accept and often blame others for their shortcomings. The key is to realize and understand this equal playing field early on. Understand it, teach it to others, and take advantage of the great gift of life you've been given.

When you understand that you are responsible for your growth, it opens the door to opportunities you may have overlooked before–opportunities that you didn't allow yourself to believe were possible. If you want to become a professional athlete, what do you need to do to get there? If you want to become a doctor or lawyer, in what areas do you need to obtain knowledge? The best question to ask yourself is, "Why not me?" What is stopping you from becoming the best in your field? What is stopping you from becoming the best version of yourself? The answer is simple, yet powerful. The answer is you. You get in your own way! Outside factors can play a role, but how you respond and move forward plays a bigger role. You have the ability to do great things.

When I hear people say that they are too dumb to understand something or that someone else is way smarter than them, it often frustrates me. In most of those situations, people have either given up on learning new information or the latter feels as though they have been given a gift of intelligence that others simply don't have. Don't believe any of that, even for a second. For the person reading this who believes you are unintelligent, think about everything you've learned up to this point in your life. Even if it doesn't seem like much, think about the ability to read or communicate through language. Language and the written word are very complex systems to learn and under-

stand. Those two intelligent acts alone set the stage for unlimited potential for you. If you can't read, that doesn't mean you can't learn.
Audiobooks and podcasts are at your fingertips. I've known very intelligent people that possessed a wealth of knowledge, but couldn't read.
You can still learn. You can always learn.

More times than not, there is someone who thinks he is smarter
than everyone else and that he's been given a gift of intelligence. Don't
let him fool you. He learned and progressed just like anyone else. Any
"smart" person I've engaged with didn't sit around watching television
all day long. She built her knowledge through reading books, engaging with other thoughtful people, and figuring things out as she went
along.

The brain is a learning machine that can and should be trained.[39]
The more you make an effort to learn, the more your brain responds.
Intelligent people are not gifted with some unreachable intelligence
that other "normal" people don't have access to. They simply have invested the time and energy to expand their reasoning and learning,
which leads to understanding more. Invest your time and energy into
learning and growth, especially learning from others' failures. You'll
be amazed at how quickly your mind will expand and adapt to the
information you consume.

SUCCESS WILL LEAD TO PLATEAUS

Finding your success in life is difficult enough, as it normally takes consistency and effort. There are countless numbers of successful people throughout history (and present day) that we can learn from. These people have made many mistakes and most are readily willing to share those experiences with those that will listen. Learning from lessons shared is a pivotal factor in advancing success in your own life. It still won't be easy because you will need to implement tough concepts and habits, but it can make things a little easier. When you receive the honor of learning from someone else, rather than spending the time figuring it out yourself, you have something greater than most people realize—you have a shortcut to success. The person teaching you has given you a savings of your most valuable resource—your time. With many wise teachers and shortcuts compounded together, you can grow at a rapid pace.

A wise person once taught me that growth is like trekking up a mountain. It can be difficult and stressful when you're going straight up. There are times when your body aches, and you don't think you can go any further. When you're in the midst of the uphill battle, it's tough to see beyond the grind. Even though you might want to press on without stopping, you can't continuously climb. It's physically impossible—you will exhaust yourself. You require rest, and you need a plateau. These plateaus allow one to rest and prepare for the next uphill climb. If there were no plateaus, there would be no strength for the next uphill climb. Take advantage of the plateaus, but don't be satisfied with one. Use your time of rest to build your strength and motivation to get to the next summit. Success is a lot like this journey as well. Once you gain the confidence and knowledge of how to do something that others may see as difficult, it becomes easier and you hit a plateau. It can become easy to you and others that know what you're doing. There's nothing wrong with that. You've worked hard to get there. You've climbed and exerted physical and mental energy to earn that plateau. Remember where you've come from and who helped you get there. Rest and prepare for your next challenge. Learn to be comfortable with the uncomfortable. Learn to look forward to your next challenge while also enjoying the fruits of your labor with those in your life.

HABITS, HABITS, HABITS

We covered this earlier in the book, but another way to make your professional failure journey a little easier is the forming of habits. These habits allow your brain to run on autopilot–you form habits whether you like it or not. They come, and they go, whether you are aware of them or not. Bad habits can be a detriment to you and those around you, but good habits can propel you forward. If you can be conscious of your habits and strive to form good habits, you will allow your mind to function at a higher level. Instead of worrying about the little things *(like where you left your keys)*, you can use your mental energy for more important tasks. If you're struggling with your keys, form a habit of putting them in the same place every time you walk in your home. It's simple, but it makes a massive difference. On average, people spend 20-30 minutes a day looking for misplaced items.[40] If you add that up over the course of a year, that means most people spend around 120-180 hours looking for misplaced items. Think of the time you could save if you even cut that in half! If you got an extra 60 hours back during the year, you could read 8-10 books. You could have time to do a simple exercise routine. Or you could just have 60 more hours to rest and catch your breath. Whatever you choose to do with that extra time, it's now available to you. But you have to be aware of your daily habits, because your daily habits control the flow of your life.

I've also learned that habits should be alive and never stagnant. There's a difference between stagnant habits and habits on autopilot. When a habit is stagnant, it's not adding value to your life or the life of others. It's a hindrance. When a good habit is alive on autopilot, it's adding value and productivity to your life and those around you–it's a positive and life-giving action. Too many stagnant habits can weigh heavy on you. Be very aware of the types of habits you create, and even after you have them down, take note of which ones add value and which ones are a hindrance. Then adjust accordingly. If your habit is adding value to your life, preserve it and keep it up. If your habit is stagnant, it might be time to reevaluate and move on.

In *The Power of Habit*, Duhigg states, "There's nothing you can't do if you get the habits right."[41] When you purposefully design your habits during the day and week, you free your mind up to focus on more difficult problems. It's nothing new, but for example, when I come home, I try to put my keys in the same place every time. This seems small, but I am very aware of all the wasted energy people use looking for small, temporarily lost items. Think of all the fights that couples get into because they blame each other for who lost the keys. And then those people go on to be agitated with someone else and it adds a negative effect on people outside the home. All from one little set of keys. One habit can have a positive snowball effect on so many things during your day. Start with one small habit and just do it. Repeat it until you don't even think about it. Then add another small habit the following week. These habits will compound quickly, free you up to focus on more important tasks, and relieve undue stress in your life. Habits can make your life easier and allow you to rest and enjoy those plateaus a little more frequently.

LACK OF KNOWLEDGE

What do you think about when you consider what you want in life? What stands in your way? No matter what it is, it most likely is linked back to a lack of knowledge. It's really nothing more than that. If you had more knowledge on how to make money or create freedom, would anything stand in your way?

Most people think that it's a money problem or a circumstance problem, but it's not. If you knew how to create a product that could be manufactured for a dollar and sold for ten dollars, you would have an opportunity. Life simply comes down to the choices you make, right or wrong. It's ultimately your responsibility. How do you go about learning and gaining the necessary knowledge you need? You sacrifice today for a better tomorrow. You sacrifice time today to read and grow so, hopefully, your life can get easier in the long run–this equates to short-term pain for long-term gains. The easier the choices you make today, the harder your life will be later on. The harder choices and sacrifices you make today can lead to an easier life down the road.

It's easier to sit around, play video games, and blackout to Netflix shows, but that's a short-term pleasure. Don't seek short-term pleasures; they almost always lead to ruin. Not to say you can't enjoy a TV show or piece of cake now and then, but don't make it a habit. Make it a special occasion. If you eat chocolate cake every day as a habit for dessert, it's going to lead to health complications. Choose habits that will lead to your long-term success, the success that you can then share abundantly with others. Sacrifice the short-term for the long-term, and you will see tremendous results. They may not come immediately, but when you wake up in five years, you will thank your old self for sacrificing so fiercely years ago.

FOCUS ON THE PROCESS

How many times have you been in a conversation with someone and she stops interacting with you to look at her smartwatch? She might have an incoming text or email notification, but it doesn't matter–she has lost focus in the conversation. A person can simply not fully listen and read at the same time. The process of checking a smartwatch in the middle of a conversation breaks the flow of the conversation. This is a big reason why I really don't like smartwatches with notifications and won't wear them. Compare this to your journey. Don't allow other things and/or people to become a smartwatch. There will always be numerous distractions, but only if you turn on notifications and allow them to rob you of your focus. Keep your focus and learn to see past distractions or temporary disappointments. The more you learn to focus, the better you'll be.

Oftentimes, when you start something new, you will have moments and days of exhaustion or you will feel defeated. Just know that you are not alone. It takes mental and physical energy to live in the present and focus on what you're doing right now. It will start to become easier as you stick with the process and persevere. Your effort will become habitual and it will require less energy to get started. It can become something you don't even think about but just do. You will learn to enjoy the process and look forward to learning new things.

If you can focus on the process, in the long run, you won't let the setbacks along the way trip you up and discourage you. The less you care about your results today, the better you will become. Your habits and processes will guide you, and your results will be a byproduct. Your results will just happen naturally.

ULTIMATE FREEDOM TO FAIL

I would certainly be negligent to not mention where the root of my freedom to fail comes from. It's not entirely from other people believing in or supporting me. And it's not from an abundance of self-esteem.

Although these things are highly important, the ultimate freedom to fail for me is found in Jesus Christ. If we fail at everything in this life but have Jesus, we still get to spend eternity in Heaven. If everything else around us falls, we still have that to hold onto. With that in mind, how can you possibly be afraid of failure?

Don't know what Jesus did for the world? Let's talk about this; it's so very important. C.S. Lewis said it well when he stated, "Christianity, if false, is of no importance, and if true, of infinite importance. The only thing it cannot be is moderately important."[42] What is it that Jesus did that was so important? In short, he sacrificed Himself to pay for the world's sins. There was a debt to be paid for sin, and Jesus took the place of you and me so that we could have eternal life with Him. God became man, lived a perfect life, and died for our sins. He was blameless and sinless, yet He was willing to sacrifice Himself so that we might have eternal life.

Once you understand the freedom that the choice of believing in Jesus brings, you can fully understand the freedom from failure that I enjoy. Can you learn from failure without knowing Jesus? Yes, but I would argue that it's a false sense of security. That security is based on others' opinions, which can be shifting sands and an inconsistent target. When you have absolute faith that nothing in this world really matters and that this earth is not your final home, you can go out and live a life of freedom. Freedom from criticisms, freedom from the fear of failure, freedom from keeping up with the Jones, and a whole host of other things. You take what comes and you learn from it, knowing that ultimately, your goal is to be the best version of yourself that God created you to be. Not for your glory but in appreciation of the gift you have been given.

WHERE DO WE GO FROM HERE?

With a new mindset and outlook, what opportunities do you look for going forward? There might be so many opportunities that you may feel overwhelmed. It's like the old quote by S. R. Parchment, *"When the pupil is ready, the master appears."*[43] When you open your eyes to the abundant resources available to you, it's life-changing. There are more mentors than people seeking mentors, and there are numerous ways to start integrating your newfound skill of learning. Remember, you can learn something new from anything around you: people, places, and things.

Think of each and every path to a better you. Not just the people around you that you have immediate access to, but think of the wisdom and growth potential when paired with modern technology. There are thousands, if not millions, of mentors right in your pocket. The smartphone you carry around gives you access to endless podcasts that you can soak up while driving, relaxing, or working out. Instead of listening to music while driving, why not put on a podcast and fill your mind with a subject you've been interested in but never took the time to learn? It's like having a mentor in your front seat with you! You don't have to mutually agree on a time to meet, you simply have 24/7 access to that mentor's brain! Podcasts aren't as good as a real life mentor, because you can't ask him questions, but you can practice the art of listening and discernment.

A step beyond podcasts may be books. Books have obviously been around for centuries, but the power contained inside good books can be more valuable than most podcasts. Good books are refined, proven, and have stood the test of time and criticism. Podcasts are great but tend to be raw and unfiltered. The content can be great, but the thinking is not as refined as books. Writing is an art. Soak up the wisdom of people that took the time and effort to write a book. It's not an easy task. If you're not into reading, the author usually has an audiobook as well! There's usually a solution to all excuses!

The next step beyond books is having a real mentor in your life: someone you can ask hard questions and talk through tough situations. You don't have to see him daily, but you do need to check in with him monthly at a minimum. Having a mentor in your life can help you learn faster and avoid a lot of costly mistakes as we've discussed in earlier chapters. The key to finding a mentor is to provide value to him and not just take his time and knowledge.

Good mentors are often successful people and highly value their time. You can try giving gifts to get his attention and then once you are granted the time to access him, ask how you can add value to his life in return for allowing you to learn under him.

There are also many situations that are nothing more than a lunch or coffee with an older, wiser person. You don't need find a mentor that has to devote daily or even weekly time to help advise you. For example, a few years back, I asked a local entrepreneur named Doug

Pitt to meet for lunch. He surprisingly said yes and we met a few weeks later. Doug explained that when he was my age an older business man sat down with him and made a big impact on the trajectory of his life. I asked him to share the best piece of investing advice he'd been given, and what he shared impacted the trajectory of my investing career and life. Doug knew I was a baseball fan, so he spoke in baseball terms. He looked me in the eyes and said, *"Focus on singles and doubles. You don't need to swing for the fences. Singles and doubles add up to runs, and then the home runs will come later."* I took what he shared to heart and have followed it as best I can ever since. One brief moment in time can have a lasting impact on you and those around you.

You never know what doors might open for you, and what incredible lessons are available in these short moments in time. Don't be afraid to ask an experienced stranger and never get discouraged if the answer is no. Sometimes it just doesn't work out but what matters is you're giving it your best effort. When we try, the world often rewards us in unexpected ways.

Lastly, remember what your most valuable resource is and will always be–*time*. Spend your time wisely and treat it with tender-loving care. The chance for effort today will never return. Make the most of right now and allow your daily actions to compound into the future.

Your future self will thank you.

ENDNOTES

1   Lubbock Online, *Former Dallas Cowboy Emmitt Smith Tells Mentor Tech Audience to Pursue Passions*, Dreams, 2017, https://www.lubbockon-line.com/local/news/2017-04-13/former-dallas-cowboy-emmitt-smith-tells-mentor-tech-audience-pursue-passions

2   Mark Koss, *Emmitt Smith Has Quite a List of Mentors*, 2021, https://www.bizjournals.com/milwaukee/news/2021/10/08/emmitt-smith-has-quite-a-list-of-mentors.html

3   Facebook Watch, *So, ever wondered what it is like to go down the rabbit hole? Well, Scott Sauls was invited in to the "secret" @RickWarren library.* https://fb.watch/7eBkKL4fii

4   Lisa M Hayes, *The Power of Self Talk*, 2017, https://www.lisamhayes.com/blog/post/the-power-of-self-talk

5   Ecclesiastes 9:14, *Berean Study Bible*, The Bible Hub, 2016, https://berean.bible/index.html

6   Anthony Moore, *How To Stop Being Afraid of Looking Stupid*, https://anthony-moore.medium.com/how-to-stop-being-afraid-of-looking-stupid-a533a8033e11

7   Jessica Hamzelou, *Your Autopilot Mode is Real - Now We Know How the Brain Does It*, 2017, https://www.newscientist.com/article/2151137-your-autopilot-mode-is-real-now-we-know-how-the-brain-does-it/

8   Sir Isaac Newton, 1675, https://www.science.edu/acellus/2018/11/newton-seeing-further

9   Homer, *The Odyssey*, London : New York, W. Heinemann; G.P. Putnam's sons, 1919.

10   Merriam-Webster, *Essential Meaning of Mentor*, https://www.merriam-webster.com/dictionary/mentor

11   Liz Wiseman with Greg McKeown, *Multipliers*, (HarperBusiness; June 15, 2010); https://thewisemangroup.com/books/multipliers

12   Epictetus, *Epictetus Quotes to Make You Think*, https://everydaypower.com/epictetus-quotes

13   Karl Smallwood, *Who Was Cunningham of Cunningham's Law?*, 2014, http://www.todayifoundout.com/index.php/2014/09/cunningham-cunninghams-law

14   Alison Pearce Stevens, *Learning Rewires the Brain*, Science News for Students, 2014, https://www.sciencenewsforstudents.org/article/learning-rewires-brain

15   Dick Ahlstrom, *Science Finds You Can Teach an Old Dog New Tricks*, 2019, https://www.irishtimes.com/business/innovation/science-finds-you-can-teach-an-old-dog-new-tricks-1.3835389

16   University of Geneva, *How Does the Brain Learn by Talking to Itself?*, 2019, https://medicalxpress.com/news/2019-01-brain.html

17 Genius Intelligence, Articles Database, http://www.geniusintelligence.com/nikolatesla.htm

18 Kate Rodriguez, *How Einstein and Edison Solved Problems in Their Sleep*, 2016, https://www.inc.com/the-muse/albert-einstein-thomas-edison-your-half-asleep-brain-can-solve-problems-better.html

19 Zig Ziglar, *See You At the Top*, 2000, https://www.amazon.com/SEE-YOU-AT-TOP-Anniversary-ebook/dp/B0047T78TQ

20 Brian Patrick Eha, *Zig Ziglar and the Importance of Helping Others*, 2012, https://www.entrepreneur.com/article/225131

21 Jim Kwik, *Limitless*, 2020, https://www.limitlessbook.com

22 Mel Schwartz L.C.S.W., *The Problem with Perfection*, 2008, https://www.psychologytoday.com/us/blog/shift-mind/200811/the-problem-perfection

23 James Hamblin, *100 Percent Is Overrated*, The Atlantic, 2015, https://www.theatlantic.com/education/archive/2015/06/the-s-word/397205

24 Cameron Norsworthy, Romper, *How Calling Your Kid Smart Could Actually Hurt Them Later In Life*, 2017 https://www.romper.com/p/telling-your-kids-theyre-smart-may-actually-make-them-bad-students-new-study-finds-2376576

25 The Spiritual Life, African Proverbs, Emphasis added, https://slife.org/african-proverbs

[26] Tim, *Descartes: I Think Therefore I Am*, Philosophy & Philosophers, May 1, 2020, https://www.the-philosophy.com/descartes-i-think-therefore-i-am

[27] Merriam-Webster, Essential Meaning of Malleble, https://www.merriam-webster.com/dictionary/malleable

[28] Bob McDonald, *Nitrous Oxide 101: The Basics Of The Gas Everyone Loves To Hate*, 2021, https://www.enginelabs.com/engine-tech/nitrous-oxide-101-the-basics-of-the-gas-everyone-loves-to-hate

[29] Napoleon Hill, *Think and Grow Rich*, 1937, https://www.barnesandnoble.com/w/think-and-grow-rich-napoleon-hill/1124936072

[30] Jessica Wei, *Money Is A Great Servant But A Bad Master – Francis Bacon,* Updated 2021, https://due.com/blog/money-is-a-great-servant-but-a-bad-master-francis-bacon

[31] George S. Clason, *The Richest Man in Babylon*, First published: 1926, https://www.amazon.com/Richest-Man-Babylon-George-Clason/dp/1505339111

[32] ESV Study Bible, English Standard Version, Crossway, 2011

[33] I can't find this video at this time. As soon as I do, I will update this footnote.

[34] Hal Elrod, *The Miracle Morning*, 2012, https://miraclemorning.com

35 Health Essentials, *Why Giving Is Good for Your Health*, 2020, https://health.clevelandclinic.org/why-giving-is-good-for-your-health

36 Charles Duhigg, *The Power of Habit*, Random House: 2012, https://charlesduhigg.com/the-power-of-habit

37 Ryan Holiday, *Ego is the Enemy*, 2016, http://egoistheenemy.com

38 Confucius, https://slife.org/quotes-from-confucius

39 Ritch Flynn, *Is The Brain A Muscle? The Truth About The Brain*, 2020, https://blog.mindvalley.com/is-the-brain-a-muscle/

40 Dana Barker Davies, *How Much Time Do You Spend Looking For Lost Possessions?*, https://www.selfgrowth.com/articles/how-much-time-do-you-spend-looking-for-lost-possessions-0

41 Charles Duhigg, *The Power of Habit*, Random House: 2012, https://charlesduhigg.com/the-power-of-habit

42 Harry Farley, *10 Times C.S. Lewis Made the Case for Christ*, 2016, https://www.christiantoday.com/article/10.times.c.s.lewis.made.the.case.for.christ/96030.htm

43 S. R. Parchment, *Steps to Self-Mastery*, 1927, https://books.google.com/books/about/Steps_to_Self_Mastery.html?id=gmtvvvEGTXAC26 Napoleon Hill, Think and Grow Rich, 1937, https://www.barnesandnoble.com/w/think-and-grow-rich-napoleon-hill/1124936072

ACKNOWLEDGMENTS

Just like anything, this book would not have been possible without the encouragement and guidance of some special people.

Kendra, thank you for taking a risk and marrying me! You are a light and a breathe of fresh air. I love learning with you. We are a true partnership and I can't imagine having to face this world without you.

Dad, you are an amazing example·to me. You set a course for my life early on, and I learned so much from you! I could not have designed a better father to learn from.

Mom, you were always there for me and taught me how to treat other people–even when I didn't agree with them. You are the best mother anyone could ask for! I'm very thankful for you.

Emily, Sarah, and Levi, we didn't always see eye-to-eye but I was pretty lucky to have such wise younger siblings. You all taught me a lot, even if you didn't realize it, and I hope that I was a positive presence in all of your lives. So proud of all of you!

Jesse, Brian, and Lindsay, all my siblings we very lucky in who they found as their partner for life! I love family gatherings and learning new things from all of you! Brian, are you up for some 10-9-8?

Meme, thank you for putting up with me! I learned so much on the farm and still love learning new things from you! Cookie nights are still some of my favorite nights with family.

Granny, you are such a rock! You not only raised my dad but you also helped keep me in line. Thank you for a great example to me.

To Papa & Grandpa, I gained so much wisdom from both of you!

I miss both of you dearly and look forward to seeing you again one day in heaven. Thank you for being such a stable example to me when I was young.

To the Williams family, thank you for welcoming me with open arms into your family! I'm very lucky to have the chance to be a part of such an incredible family unit.

To all my cousins, thanks for being such great companions at family gatherings. I've learned countless things from all of you, younger and older. I'm very lucky to have family like you.

To all my aunts and uncles, thanks for putting up with me! I know I was a curious kid and you had every right to constantly banish me to the corner–but thankfully you didn't! The wisdom you've shared with me is priceless. Thank you for taking the time to invest in one of your irritating little nephews!

Nick Johnson, who sent me a text asking about my progress virtually every morning during my writing time. Even when I didn't feel like writing it was an encouragement to see his text waiting for me on my phone.

Brandi Kepli, who helped edit and revise this book. Thank you for being patient with my lack of writing skills! I know I've improved from the time your feedback began.

Ashley Bunting, thank you for guiding me through the publishing process at Merack! I would have been lost without our weekly meetings that kept us on track. Thank you!

Acknowledgements

Made in the USA
Middletown, DE
05 July 2022

68490868R00118